Dr Lisa Dethridge has twenty years' experience writing for film, television and print in Australia and the United States. During this time she has worked with producers and writers in both countries, and for major and independent studios and networks. Her clients include Fox, Warner, Working Title, MTV, CBS, NBC, CNN, Granada, SBS, the Australian Film Commission and ABC Australia. She has written about the screen for magazines and journals, including a regular column for *Vogue Australia*. She has taught writing and media/communications at the American Film Institute, the Writers Program at the University of California, Los Angeles, New York University, the Australian Film, Television and Radio School, the Royal Melbourne Institute of Technology and the University of Melbourne. She has a PhD in Media Ecology from New York University.

Much of the material in this book forms part of the online course in Screenwriting run by the Australian Film, TV and Radio School. See www.AFTRS.edu.au

Writing your SCREENPLAY

Dr Lisa Dethridge

ALLEN&UNWIN

AFTRS

First published in 2003

Copyright © Lisa Dethridge 2003

Allen & Unwin
83 Alexander Street
Crows Nest NSW 2065
Australia
Phone: (61 2) 8425 0100
Fax: (61 2) 9906 2218
Email: info@allenandunwin.com
Web: www.allenandunwin.com

National Library of Australia
Cataloguing-in-Publication entry:

Dethridge, Lisa.
   Writing your screenplay.

   Includes index.
   ISBN 1 74114 083 8.

   1. Motion picture authorship. I. Title.

808.23

Set in 10/15 pt Veljovic Book by Bookhouse, Sydney
Printed by Griffin Press, Adelaide

10 9 8 7 6 5 4 3 2 1

The author acknowledges the assistance of colleagues Kathy Mueller and Simon Britton at the Australian Film, Television and Radio School and Malcolm King at RMIT University.

This book is dedicated to my children, Lucian and Ava.

Contents

Introduction

Why write for the screen?

So you want to write a screenplay? You may be working in the industry or hoping to join the ranks. You may be shooting your own film or just watching other people's. You may be burning to visit Cannes with a script in your hand or writing your latest novel. Whether you're a film professional, a student or a film buff with a powerful urge to write, this book can help you achieve your aims by providing a technical foundation for creativity.

The screenplay often begins as a personal idea—the passionate outcome of a writer's solitary labour or as a collaboration between a writer and another writer, director or producer. The finished screenplay then becomes the property of a large group of collaborators (producer, director, cast and crew) who take the writer's blueprint, the script, and construct it on screen for an audience.

Within this process, the writer must be both an artist and a technician. One who 'speaks' a language that transcends both art and industry.

Many nations have contributed to the evolution of popular, mainstream cinema. Europe, India, Russia, Iran, China, Japan and Australia have each developed signature styles that capture audiences both locally and world-wide. This book encourages you to explore techniques and issues that may be part of these diverse narrative or storytelling traditions. At the same time, it offers technical guidance from the classic Hollywood codes and conventions that will help you estimate how an audience may 'read' your work. Films discussed in detail throughout the following chapters include *The Matrix, Run Lola Run, Pulp Fiction, Basic Instinct, Breakfast at Tiffany's, Psycho, Sliding Doors, Thelma & Louise, The Silence of the Lambs, Star Wars* and many more.

Different audiences need different things. Urban tribes of western 'consumers' may like stories to reflect the fast-paced frenzy of life in late capitalist society. For example, in recent hit screenplays such as *The Matrix* and *Run Lola Run,* we see a new, fragmented approach to the traditional story 'world'. Such stories manipulate the time frames of the narrative to create a kind of synchronicity between characters and events. This technique allows the audience to pause and examine how different characters cope with the same situations from different viewpoints.

This kind of complexity reflects the information-dense reality (or realities) that people now inhabit, especially in urban societies. It may also reflect the increasingly global influence of ancient world-views such as those of the great Hindu and Buddhist traditions. As a result of this wider philosophical perspective, much new cinema suggests that our view of ourselves in space and time may be evolving beyond a strictly linear perspective. It is a radical view which seems to indicate that we each inhabit a series of parallel universes. That we all create different imaginative versions of ourselves that may be at odds with our everyday reality.

While the young and the computer-literate are moving swiftly toward such expansive imaginary states, the more general international audience may still be attuned to traditional linear forms, where the beginning, the middle and the end of a story follow in simple, logical order. Any radical departure from this framework may therefore need to be made very skilfully, providing the audience with firm anchor points along the way. The more familiar the writer is with classic storytelling blueprints, the more likely they are to make successful departures from the norm.

This book is designed to nurture your ideas for innovative cinema. It is designed for writers who may want to tell stories about people and things that are often miles away from mainstream traditions. As screenwriters, we can create cinema that draws people together from different language and culture backgrounds. To achieve this ideal, we will focus on storytelling techniques that are recognised the world over due to their clarity and resonance. While some of these techniques derive from a western framework, we encourage you to question the assumptions underlying them; assumptions about the role of the writer, the role of the audience and the nature of good storytelling.

An Iranian film called *A Time for Drunken Horses* by Bahman Ghobadi won the prestigious Camera D'Or prize at Cannes 2000. It is the first film ever made in the Khurdish language and tells the simple but gut-wrenching story of a refugee family who struggle to survive on the fringes of civilisation. The success of this film around the world suggests that film can make the boundaries between diverse cultures seem transparent, regardless of politics, religion and geography.

What about your role as storyteller? What is driving you to write in the first place? The urge to tell stories has complex roots in human psychology and behaviour. In sharing our experience with others, we feel the reassurance and comfort of the tribe. We may also instruct, entertain and amuse.

Some suggest the best writing comes from anger; from 'the fire in the belly' of one who has an urgent need to communicate to others. Some suggest that writers should write what they know and stick to the familiar worlds of their immediate reality. Others suggest the sky is the limit and that cinema can conquer all constraints of space and time. One underlying theme of this book is that today's screenwriters are developing a new sense of the time/space continuum. Our sense of the relationship between screen time/space and real time/space may now reflect our understanding of the world as one involving parallel universes, parallel realities and even virtual reality.

Regardless of which 'reality' you inhabit, you can use this book to help you focus on the most appropriate type of story to match your talents: your message and your level of development. You might be a passionate person with plenty to say and a head full of exciting images. Are you ready to pin down these passions and ideas in the form of a screenplay?

While this book provides a practical program for the creation of screenplay material, it also raises larger questions about the ongoing evolution of screen storytelling and the position of screenwriting in relation to other arts. It provides a comprehensive overview of this fast-growing field while offering practical guidance and exercises tailored around specific goals.

We look at authors whose practical guides to screenwriting have become part of standard industry vocabulary. Syd Field and Linda Seger, for example, both provide logical and sturdy templates for the understanding of three act structure. Robert McKee explores various tools at the screenwriter's disposal while Chris Vogler refers to the psychology of Carl Jung and the anthropology of Joseph Campbell to provide workable templates for narrative and character.

In later chapters we will examine the important ideas of these authors and of anthropologists and psychologists, who suggest that we tell stories in response to basic human needs. Our stories reflect our hopes of finding the meaning of life, of finding answers to the big questions—who am I? What am I doing here and why? This search for meaning is often tied up with an ethical evaluation of events as we humans want to understand events in order to know how to respond to them. The writer's job is to make this complex process both manageable and entertaining for the audience.

This book will encourage you to focus and organise ideas that may otherwise feel chaotic and outside your control. By structuring your vision in a step-by-step way, the rush of images and concepts can be 'captured' and tamed, ready for the page, ready for the camera's eye.

Finding interesting stories may not be a problem for you. Most writers have several characters and story ideas rattling about in their imagination. Many have files full of fabulous story outlines, magazine articles and notes. Not all of these stories are appropriate for translation to the screen, however. Identifying and selecting story material for different media and markets is a skill that takes time to develop.

Aspiring writers may find it easy and fun to come up with great movie ideas in the solitude of a rainy afternoon at their desk or with friends over coffee. Your own personal experience, your passion for writing or for film, will tell you that stories are to be found everywhere. The hard task is actually sitting down and writing one hundred sparkling pages of screenplay-format material.

Whether you are juggling an excess of story ideas or struggling to focus on one, we will cover some of the complex imaginative challenges that help a writer to focus on what stories are most appropriate for them. We then move forward in a work-like way, building your screenplay from the ground up.

When revising your ideas for story material, it is worth examining your own ambitions as a screenwriter.

- What do you hope to achieve by writing for the screen?
- What do you hope to explore and understand as part of your research for the project?
- What are the key ideas and images that move you to communicate with others?
- What is the 'voice' you hope to cultivate for this communication?
- What is the genre or story type you wish to use as your vehicle?

Spend some time exploring these questions on paper. Try to focus on the key elements of your own experience as an artist who has something to share with an audience. Focus on stories, images and worlds that are most appropriate to your project.

The following chapters will help you to select and develop the right story for the right audience. They will also help you to commit to that story so you can see the process through from start to finish; to develop its contours and flesh out its characters with all the energy and craft skills required to produce a working screenplay document. If you are in touch with your passions from the start, you are more likely to produce a work that is lively and relevant to the audience.

Each chapter of this book concludes with one or more exercises which guide you in the process of preparing a screen story. By completing these exercises, you may create the necessary outlines and 'treatment' documents required to construct a screenplay of short or full 'feature' length.

The guidelines and examples offered here are intended to help each writer to explore the classical past of story structure and to glimpse the future. We discuss the classical 'unities' of space, as well as alternative models for screen drama.

You will also achieve a high level of craft competency based on solid techniques including:

- a basic technical proficiency in storytelling for the screen
- a toolbox of proven techniques and exercises
- basic fluency in film language and structural analysis
- confidence in your abilities to conceive and write screenplay materials.

For now, we are steering a straight course towards the classic conventions of screenwriting form. Later chapters examine more radical examples of contemporary screenwriting that bend or break with convention. The future belongs to those writers who can grasp these rules and then break them confidently and gracefully, with full audience approval.

Essential tools for screenplay development

The final chapters of this book offer solid guidelines to assist with the writing of good dialogue and well-constructed scenes. There are also guidelines for the writing of scene breakdowns and outlines that help the writer to put their screenplay document together in a logical fashion. While we cover the 'nuts and bolts' of the screenplay form in great detail, the more important area for exploration is the conceptual underpinning that exists 'off the page' of the script itself.

The first half of this book outlines several important conceptual structures that enable you to build a strong story world and believable characters. These structures also allow you to connect with an audience and maintain their interest. The key to this process lies in what we will call 'the four Ps'. The process hinges on the main character, also known as (1) the *protagonist*. This character must be sympathetic or appealing, and must move (2) the *plot* forward by grappling with (3) a dramatic *problem*. These technical elements are unified under (4) the *premise*. This fourth P represents your passion as a writer; it is the heart and soul of the story, the central unifying concept or philosophy that governs its various themes.

The exercises and concepts outlined in following chapters focus on these four structures. When thinking of your protagonist, you will consider their inner world or psychology. What drives or motivates this main character? What is their key goal? Their biggest fear? Their biggest problem? Having figured out what makes the protagonist 'tick', you can select the key moments or events that will reflect and materialise images of these goals and fears. Eventually, you will turn these images into scenes that will become turning points in your plot. The story then becomes a kind of game for the audience, where they observe and participate with the protagonist as this character goes about the business of solving their main problem. Their performance will depend on the kind of psychology you equip them with.

The writer must keep the game moving forward by organising all the cause-and-effect relations between characters, locations and events within a schedule of scenes that unfolds over the course of 90 minutes or so. This means that the writer must consider which events and moments of the protagonist's story they wish to reveal and which can remain 'off screen'.

Time is the basic building block of cinema. In order to substitute one set of events (reality) for another (film reality), the screenwriter, like the composer, must play tricks with the audience's perception of time. This is more than 'passing the time'; it is about creating various illusions. The pacing of the story should be set up to gain the interest of the audience early in the piece (preferably in the first five to ten minutes), then to build audience interest while moving swiftly towards an inevitable conclusion. (Inevitable because it has been planned by the writer from page 1 of the script.)

The screenplay is written like a symphony that must account for many moods, locations and voices. The screenplay is also like an architect's blueprint in that it encodes and describes the complex transformation of an idea into the production of a massive entity. The film itself is like a building. It is constructed by the director, cast and crew from the written instructions of the screenwriter, or story architect. Like a building, the film is 'inhabited' by the audience, who move through it visually and imaginatively.

Your challenge as a screenwriter is to use all the visual and aural potential of the medium to make the audience recognise emotions and ideas that may otherwise remain unseen or unspoken. The screenwriter has two main vehicles for the creation of onscreen tension and conflict. These are (1) the dialogue and (2) the action.

Say, for instance, you need to create a scene to describe a character's inner loneliness and grief. You might set the scene in a rainy cemetery where the protagonist cries alone, or you might set it at a noisy birthday celebration, where the character is clearly lost, despite the party of joyful people around her. While both scenes may express a similar idea, each produces a remarkably different tone and mood. One is about solitude; the other is about being alone in a crowd.

Both the inner, psychological, and the outer, physical, worlds of the protagonist may be organised by the writer according to themes. These themes help us to focus on a particular set of concerns or ideas. A good writer then organises and edits their themes according to a single, governing concept or premise. Having a strong, driving idea behind the work helps the writer to limit what can otherwise be an overwhelming amount of ideas and material. For instance, if the writer knows that their premise concerns the pain of solitude, they may choose the cemetery scene in the example above. On the other hand, the writer's premise may concern our ability to feel alone despite, or perhaps because of, being surrounded by others. Then the writer may choose the second option to express that idea more succinctly.

Creating a screenwriting folio

The screenplay itself represents the final stage in a long research and writing process, which often begins on the pages of notebooks and journals. The writer needs to keep a journal handy for the many notes you will make on the purpose of your story. Before you begin the screenplay itself, you may write down the reasons why the story is important, why it is different, or why it is similar to other stories told on film. You may note ideas and images, make sketches or keep photos which inspire you to write background material on your story world.

You may also use your journal to explore the psychology of yourself as writer (why must I write this?), as well as that of your protagonist and main characters. You may use the folio to write research notes on the history, or 'backstory', of your story world: on the locations, and the special occupations and quirks of the characters. Ask yourself how you may use each of these elements to add meaning and colour to your story.

This preparatory material is best written before the process of drafting the main plotlines and scene breakdowns. Then, when it comes time to begin the outlines and draft of your screenplay document, you will have a large body of work to refer to as a guide to the underlying concepts, ideas and images that will make your story world seem real and convincing to an audience.

In the television industry, those producing TV series usually have a large body of reference material on hand to use in the story department as plots are being developed. Each TV series usually has its own set of notes about the 'world' and characters of the ongoing story. This reserve of ideas is known as 'the bible'. The series bible provides a set of documents about the original concept that drives the story and the main characters. It outlines the basic logic of the series world and can be used by different writers to ensure that there is consistency in the treatment of the story, despite changes to writing staff.

This all suggests that a screenwriter needs to manage a large folio of research notes, scenes and pages. Like the novelist, the screenwriter must be prolific—they must be able to generate pages and pages of written work. The finished draft of a screenplay is a slim volume that may only amount to 100 or so pages. However, to achieve this result, the screenwriter may generate a research folio of twice or three times that size in the form of character notes, story ideas and background material for the work. The screenwriter will also go over their screenplay many times in order to get the details right. So, in the end, there is a lot more writing required of the writer than a mere 100 or so pages of finished script.

The exercises at the end of each chapter are designed to get you into the swing of habitual writing. They are based around the creation of your screenwriting folio. You may be building on these notes daily, so keep them handy.

Before you start reading Chapter 1, pause for a moment and consider—it is not enough just to *think* about a character and story. Some people call themselves writers but don't actually write. Such 'writers' think beautiful thoughts; they have brilliant inspirations; they go to cafés and articulate their fine ideas. This is all a valid part of your early research phase and may involve quite a bit of dreaming as you try to conjure up images of your characters and their situations.

Good writing is the end of a lengthy thought process. However, there is a danger that the aspiring writer can fall into the pose of a 'wanna-be writer' and talk a lot about ideas, rather than actually writing them. The *real writer* goes home after the café and pins these beautiful thoughts down on paper. A work-like writer will do more than imagine a fascinating story world; they will *write down* what they envisage to be the tiny details of this world. A 'wanna-be' will stay up late, chatting with their pals about their 'work'. In contrast, the real writer sits at home and actually performs the task in a focused way, transforming abstract ideas and images into written language that can be shared with others through media such as film, video and print.

In creating a screenwriting folio, you are providing yourself with a rich context or platform for creativity. Without a reserve of themes, characters and location notes, the writer has no basic building material to work with. Use your journal to write extra, detailed material on the world of the story. Use it to explore the ideas it involves, as well as character biography and psychology. This creative process ensures that the writer knows the story world and the characters that inhabit it. Without this in-depth research, the scenario will inevitably lack the authenticity of 'real life' and the drama will feel thin.

Your journal or folio is like 'the bible' of your screenplay. It provides you with a fundamental set of guidelines, based on solid character psychology, a credible backstory and a watertight premise. You can refer to these notes at any time in the screenwriting process to remind yourself of the basic logic and purpose of your project. The journal will also help you to stay on track and remain consistent with your aims and aspirations as a writer.

The initial stage of your screenwriting project is simple. Your aim is to satisfy your personal artistic urges in selecting the appropriate story material—characters, themes, images and locations. The next general aim is also quite simple: to generate pages. It's a good plan to develop the habit of writing a little every day, rather than wait in vain for 'inspiration' to strike. Writing is a job—if you wait for your muse to visit, you have an excuse *not* to write. If your attitude is work-like and no-nonsense, you are more likely to succeed.

1

Cinema creates a parallel universe

Chapter objectives
To balance the demands of art, the industry and the market; to explore aspects of the film industry; and to know what makes an audience tick.

Good films transport their audience into a new space/time continuum. In one sense, writing for the screen is like creating a new universe, with its own laws of space, time, and human behaviour and psychology. Your screenplay can be the blueprint for a whole new world. For the audience, a simple trip to view such a film can almost be like entering a parallel universe.

In creating good screenplays, the writer is really 'playing god' in that universe. The writer has to create an entire reality from the ground up; an imaginary world where the 'normal' constraints of space, time, behaviour and psychology no longer apply.

Like the painter, the poet and the photographer, the screen-writer needs to be a good observer. Your task is to isolate key images and events from the chaotic continuum of 'real life', and to select and edit these moments so that they express, in a fraction of 'real time', the essence of your idea.

The cinema has long been a special place in human culture. It is a realm where anything can happen, a realm comparable with the temples and theatres of the ancient world where the boundaries between our real world and our fantasy worlds are often very blurred. In this imaginary space, we are given the opportunity to assess and reassess the rituals that make up our daily lives.

To achieve this miracle, this triumph of magic over matter, a bargain must be struck between the creators of the spectacle and the audience. Part of the bargain is that the audience simply deny or forget the daily reality that exists outside the cinema. They 'suspend disbelief' in illusion and replace 'real time' with the 'reel time' provided by the film-makers. They go along for the 'ride' or journey.

To achieve their part of the bargain, the successful screenwriter must be a great seducer. They must persuade an entire audience that the 'reality' of their story is more attractive than others on offer in the cinemas next door.

If the film is a success, the audience will suspend disbelief and remain unaware of time passing in the real world outside. This is the audience's delight—to suspend their participation in the real world outside and to enter the magic realm of an imaginary zone.

As the great surrealist, the Spanish auteur Luis Buñuel pointed out, the cinema is indeed a place of dreams:

> In the hands of a free spirit the cinema is a magnificent and dangerous weapon. It is the superlative medium through which to express the world of thought, feeling and instinct . . . its way of functioning is most reminiscent of the work of the mind during sleep. A film is like . . . a dream. (1978, p. 107).

Buñuel even observed that the furnishings inside the cinema are often red, to create a womb-like sense of security and warmth, where the audience's dreams can flourish. The real world is ritualistically excluded from the draped cinema, to create an enchanted, imaginary zone envisaged first by the writer and then made manifest by the director, cast and crew.

The demands of art, the industry and the market

As the writer of a successful screenplay, you must be in control of the audience's collective dream. What will the dream look like? Who is going to pay for it all? To approach these difficult questions, let's first consider the job description of a screenwriter. Any of the following may apply:

- a highly skilled literary technician who manipulates literary structures
- a magician who creates illusions of drama and comedy on screen
- a witness to the historical events and mood of the day
- a mouthpiece for the people
- someone who uses writing as a form of art
- someone who uses writing as therapy, to express personal ideas, problems and convictions
- someone who holds up a mirror to the audience, reflecting their hopes, fears and dreams.

Wherever you fit on this scale, this book will tend to steer you towards a kind of middle road. You don't have to be a genius to write good material. Writing is a craft that can be learned, so let's not focus on your ego, your talent or your emotional status. This process isn't about therapy; it isn't about helping you to be a better human being. Of course, the act of writing can certainly be used to achieve such ends, but this isn't one of our specific aims here.

Writing that is based on ego may actually get in the way of producing a good story that is suited for a large audience. A good writer must of course cherish personal convictions, but it is equally important that the writer focus on the act of seduction that wins an audience in the first place. This means we need to develop skills in persuasion and in direct communication with others. Sometimes it is necessary to detach from one's ego and emotions in order to achieve this.

Rather than seeing writing as a form of personal therapy, let's consider the screenwriter as one who has potential in a professional, industrial environment. Within this environment, your job is to observe the tools and conventions of your craft. Having learned the craft, you are then free to construct whatever ideas you please, but always putting the audience first. This doesn't mean that you must put your own ideas last, but rather that you learn to present your ideas in such a way that they will be received and understood rather than rejected.

In Hollywood, executives refer to a good screenplay as one with 'heart'. This is shorthand for an idea that resonates on a deep emotional level with a wide range of people. To achieve this sense of 'heart', there must be a strong emotion at the centre of your story and this emotion usually comes from a writer who has a strong attitude or viewpoint to 'prove' or illustrate in their story. Some say that the best writing comes from anger, from a fire in the belly. The exercise at the end of this chapter can help you to identify the factors that are motivating you to write. It can also help you to get in touch with your strongest emotions. For now, however, let's keep an eye on the business of film-making and on how this may affect your endeavours as a screenwriter.

Understanding the industry

The film industry varies from continent to continent but tends to obey laws that were established early last century in the United States and Western Europe. French film theorist André Bazin described the evolution of the film industry according to the demands of both commercialism and the audience.

> In 1895, no one could say what films should look like or how they should go about the business . . . By 1915 the original freedom of the art was vastly restricted while its powers of expression had miraculously developed. Cinema exchanged variety for a standard form and gained eloquence as a result. It chose a few of its infinite options and these few options became the 'Cinema' we all recognise. (1976, p. 174).

Bazin pointed to various conventions that became standard during the early 20th century, including the running time of feature-length films which remains at around 80–120 minutes. It is clear that cinema is indebted to ancient forms of opera, theatre, painting and poetry for many of its formal conventions, both dramatic and visual. According to Bazin, such conventions are 'an inseparable part of our notion of cinema'. He reminds us that they are also a product of 'the institutionalisation of the art', an art that is equally influenced by business and commerce.

British film historian David Bordwell suggests that most of the standards of Western film language were formed in the early to mid-20th century. He suggests that writers today must observe narrative or storytelling conventions that first solidified between 1915 and 1938 (before World War Two) and which became further codified by Hollywood during the 'golden' epoch of American film-making in the 1940s and 50s. (Bordwell and Thompson 2001). European 'new wave' and avant-garde film-makers such as Jean Luc Godard enjoyed smashing these conventions in the 1960s, creating a new genre—the art-house film. However, such art-house films never attract the same large audiences as those using the standard 'grammar' of classic film language. Bearing this in mind, we can observe the classic conventions that are still influential today. A knowledge of these rules and codes will still inform the approach of any screenwriter, no matter how rebellious or avantgarde.

The basic economy of film

It is also worthwhile observing the basic economy that affects a screenwriter. While it costs no money to write a screenplay, the economy of film production requires three kinds of crucial investment:

- cash investment from a producer
- cash investment from an audience
- emotional investment from the audience.

Your screenplay can only be realised as a film after some very big cash investments from producers. Producers tend to invest in screenplays that seem likely to attract a large cash-paying public; this is how producers recoup their funds. A successful screenplay also requires the audience to make an emotional investment in the story and its themes. Without an interest in or attraction to your story, an audience probably won't pay cash to see it. Producers have all this in mind when assessing screenplay material. With these three forms of investment in place, the screenwriter therefore has a better chance of 'selling' their screenplay.

The simple truth is that film-making, like all the arts, has a glut of willing creative suppliers, with not enough paid work to go around. Only a small fraction of the screenplays that are written and submitted for production ever make it to the big screen. Saying you want to sell your screenplay is a little like saying you want to be a movie star. The competition is enormous and the odds are stacked against you.

The great success stories in film often come from writers who begin with small films, especially shorts, that make it into international festivals. When starting from scratch, with no experience, writers may get involved in the film industry by producing or writing a film for a limited audience of friends or family. Writing for short films or for amateur groups is a great way of creating a track record, gaining experience and getting 'a name' in the business.

It is possible to produce small films on a shoestring, and this is an area where new writers can have great success. You can provide scripts to film students or amateurs, shoot on home video, or put your own small studio of film-workers together as a means of getting your script off the ground.

Doing any kind of work within a commercial production arena is also a great way of making contacts and learning about the inner workings of film and television. If you get an 'in' to the industry by sweeping floors, you need to be confident that hard work and talent will soon find you working in a more interesting department. It makes sense to undergo an apprenticeship within the industry, rather than trying to 'crack it' as an outsider. In these ways, writers and creators gain useful contacts and experience and achieve access to the larger marketplace.

To really focus your writing skills, work through the exercises in this book and read as many screenplays as you can. The best way to get a sense of how to write a good screenplay is to examine as many fine examples of the craft as possible. You need to get a sense of what good dialogue looks like on the page—how much is too much or too little? What do effective stage directions look like? How to tell if act two is too long? The exercise at the end of chapter two will give you some ideas on how to keep an active log book of your readings. Later chapters go into the details of plot, character and scene construction.

What makes your audience tick?

Writers with ambitions in the large, commercial arena need to comprehend the workings of a multimillion-dollar industry driven by box-office attendance. This kind of writer needs to write with a large audience in mind. To survive in the brutally competitive marketplace, your story needs to attract both a producer and an audience.

One part of the writer's brief is to imagine how their story can 'find' an audience. How can you lure people into the cinema? Imagine yourself with a sandwich board outside the local movie-house. What will draw people inside to pay their hard-earned cash for the privilege of watching your material? To answer this 'bottom-line' question, you need to understand what brings an audience into the cinema in the first place.

21

What motivates people to go and see a film? This isn't a simple question. To answer it, the writer must gain access to the touchstones of human existence. For this reason, a good writer must be a little like a philosopher: one who understands the workings of the human heart. A good writer is one who knows what makes an audience tick.

A writer also needs to know what kind of audience 'belongs' to your material. Unless the audience 'invests' in your story, your screenplay simply won't work. Producers understand this and won't invest their cash unless they recognise a writer who has really thought carefully about why an audience will care about their script.

Think about your potential audience. Consider what you have to tell them that they may not have heard before.

- Who are your audience—age, interests, location?
- What would you like to tell them?
- What will draw them to your work?
- What are they looking for?

Some of the factors which bring audiences into the cinema or the video store include the following:

- to escape mundane cares
- to alleviate boredom
- to pass the time
- to create a liberation from their daily reality
- to be reassured that love and beauty exist in the world
- to engage in fantasies of sex and violence, thrills and spills
- to seek a solution to their everyday problems
- to take a 'trip' to some location or engage in an activity they have never known

- to learn about areas of human life that are attractive, exotic or forbidden.

What makes a good story?

The journey of an imaginary protagonist struggling with a problem has been driving plots since cave people daubed their caves with paintings of the bison hunt. By ritually enacting or rehearsing human actions and problems in an artistic realm, we not only relive the excitement of the moment, we also come up with solutions for real life. In painting the hunt we came to understand it.

Storytelling in cinema incorporates different cultural histories. Let's look at screenwriting within a global perspective. How are we to understand the many, diverse audiences for world cinema? Whether they realise it or not, audiences today are a part of various intertwined traditions in storytelling that go back to the time before Christ. Some tribes relate to the biblical form of parables and gospels; some to the Koran or the teachings of Confucius. Other tribes relate to the wondrous Hindu cycle, to African fables, or to the myths and legends of ancient Egyptian, Greek, Roman and Byzantine cultures.

The conventions that govern film narrative are also intertwined with those of other media, such as theatre, opera, photography, poetry and fine art. These conventions in image and story, as well as the tools used to convey them, stretch far back in time, from the computer to celluloid to the printing press and right back to cave-painting.

No matter what their influences or their audience, the writer's first priority is to create an elegant story. A messy storyline will

23

disappoint or even anger an audience, who may give it bad 'word of mouth', telling their friends not to bother seeing it.

A good story can easily be repeated or retold. In fact, the simplest test of a good story is whether or not it can be retold easily. That's why, in a pitch situation, when a writer is trying to 'sell' an idea, the producer will be looking for a story with a 'hook' that can be easily encapsulated and communicated in one line.

Robert Altman's film *The Player* gives wonderful insights into the world of the commerical screenwriter. In the opening scene, a variety of writers pitch their stories to a producer. They each mention other movies as a way of describing their script. One writer envisages her story as a vehicle for the actress Goldie Hawn: 'It's like "Goldie goes to Africa". She's found by this tribe of small people and she becomes worshipped . . .' The producer interrupts her pitch asking, 'Oh, so it's like *The Gods Must be Crazy* only the coke bottle is a movie actress?' 'Right,' the writer agrees, 'exactly. It's like *Out of Africa* meets *Pretty Woman!*

Screenwriters will often describe their work according to previous hits as a kind of shorthand technique to convey a sense of content, genre and tone. Can you image what the following film story ideas may 'look' like?

- *High Noon* as a musical
- *Apocalypse Now* set in Bosnia 2000
- *Jaws* set on a spaceship
- *The Magnificent Seven* go to Jamaica
- *Dirty Harry* with a *Terminator* twist

If a story is so obscure, complicated or ambiguous that it can not be easily summarised or repeated, it isn't a good bet for the screen. The largest outlines of the story—its central themes and the central dilemma for the main character—should be clearly drawn for the audience to follow. Otherwise, confusion can occur.

A story needs a clearly identified main character, along with clear outlines and themes, in order to 'hook' the audience and get their interest. The story must also resonate on a number of levels—mythic, cultural, psychological and artistic.

The key to high-quality story material is found in:

- the choice of subject matter and themes
- the degree of technical skill used to create the structure or framework of the story.

Good screenplays are written around invisible, inner structures that help the audience to navigate their way through the story. In Chapter 2, we discuss this technical framework according to four main categories known as 'the four Ps'—protagonist, dramatic problem, plot and premise. For now, let's focus on how to select and identify good story material.

In order to meet commercial selection criteria, a good screenplay needs to be timely. It may be relevant to today's audience and to current issues, or it may refer to classic, eternal or timeless themes such as war and peace, the follies of love, the grandeur of nature and so on. In any case, the writer must create a context for the audience to invest in on an emotional level. Only then will a producer and audience invest in the story on a financial level.

Connecting with an audience

One way of establishing firm contact with an audience is to consider universal themes that can work across different cultures and age groups. By 'universal', we mean images and ideas that will appeal to all people at all time, regardless of their race, class or religion.

It always helps a writer to consider the things we all have in common. One of these universal factors is the physical body; the body which needs to be fed, sheltered and maintained in good health. We all need food, water and a roof over our head. Stories that focus on these basic needs are sure to reach a wide variety of people in the audience. No matter what age, race, class or religion a character may be, if we see them on screen, suffering a serious disease, we will relate to them directly as a fellow human.

Other universal factors include our need to bond with others and to form groups; to make love and find shelter. Every person on the planet needs to belong with others in a tribe or group or community. Other universal needs include our need to achieve clear aims and goals, to be recognised by others, and to know and understand others. Because these needs have remained constant in all cultures over all time, they make a good starting point for storytellers. These needs are a sure 'hit' with a wide variety of people in the audience; everyone can relate to the image of a character with a broken leg, just as they can relate to the character with a broken heart.

Psychologist Abraham Maslow points to a hierarchy of human needs which structure our lives through various levels. The core of any good dramatic situation is usually concerned with these needs:

- the need for survival
- the need for safety and security
- the need for love and belonging
- the need for esteem and self-respect
- the need for fulfilment and self-actualisation.

This hierarchy reveals what motivates us and what may be at stake if our basic needs are not met. For instance, your characters will develop behaviour and coping strategies around these needs. In working with these elements, you can provide the audience with realistic characters who are driven by strong motivation.

How to create a timely story

Screenwriters need to work with good story material. It's lucky for them that interesting stories are plentiful and can be found every day in our daily experiences, in myth and folklore, in the anecdotes of friends, in newspapers and magazines, and in classic tales ready to be retold. In fact, one could say that 'good stories grow on trees'.

The economy of film production relies partly on the willingness of an audience to 'buy' one story over another. This introduces us to the concept of 'timeliness'. Audience appeal is partly a function of the mood or spirit of the times. Some stories are more appropriate to the times than others.

Contrary to myths about the industry, film producers are not always primarily concerned with the novelty of a story idea. They may often be even more attracted to classic or familiar ideas and themes that are 'tried and true'. That's why stories that follow the patterns of certain genres or types of story usually feel 'familiar' to an audience who expects, and then recognises, certain images or ideas that may belong to that genre.

In order to understand the audience—their problems, hopes, dreams and fears—it's important for the writer to be in touch with the Zeitgeist, or spirit of the times. In fact, the screenwriter must be slightly ahead of the times. Considering that it takes a few years to get a script into production after it has been sold, the writer must actually have a grip on what *tomorrow's* mood may be.

To ensure their place in this ever-changing marketplace, the writer needs to be on the crest of the new wave of oncoming ideas. For instance, in the 1990s, there was an explosion in 'gender-bender' stories that included themes of cross-dressing and drag-queens. Some writers in the early 1990s were ahead of social movements and were able to predict the oncoming spirit of the time. At this time, several hits appeared with the same theme: 'Guy meets gal, only to learn that gal is a guy (or guy is a gal)' Films such as *The Crying Game, Madame Butterfly, Boys Don't Cry, Mrs. Doubtfire* and *The Adventures of Priscilla, Queen of the Desert* have all won a swag of international awards and topped box-office listings.

It's easy to see that, while it was popular at the time, this 'gender-bender' theme is no longer 'hot'. It may no longer excite producers to read stories based on such themes, as they were so well explored in this rash of 1990s hits. Future writers will no doubt revisit the theme, but for the moment it seems to have been exhausted or absorbed by the mainstream and is no longer 'timely'.

Like fashion designers and other popular artists, the screenwriter must be aware of ideas, trends and events before they actually happen. In having to predict and evaluate the ups and downs of the cultural calendar, you must be something of a prophet or soothsayer. Your story may need to be appropriate to the audience's present concerns but within a slightly futuristic time frame. What's hot today may no longer feel relevant in five years' time.

For this reason, screenwriters often need to be aware of social and cultural undercurrents—the ideas and themes that may be bubbling just under the surface of popular awareness. The writer may work with classic favourite themes, or may find a fresh idea appropriate to audiences of the near future. It's fine to challenge the limits of the genre, but let's avoid being too risky or 'out there'. You want to entice an audience and a producer to your work, not scare them off.

Writing the 'period' film

If you are planning to write a story set in, say, the 16th century, you may find it hard to find a producer willing to invest in your project. One reason is that yesterday's mood and locations are extremely expensive to create, requiring costumes, sets and props that need much research to produce. Such films may also be challenging to a film audience that is usually focused on today's world and its mood. For these reasons, 'period' stories are harder to sell.

In order to succeed, writers of 'period' stories must identify classic themes that are as relevant to an audience today as they were in the past. Historical stories are thus a tougher challenge for writers than contemporary stories, which have the instant appeal of the 'here and now'.

Finding the 'hook'

Writers sometimes can use a snappy one-liner—a clever phrase or slogan—as a kind of shorthand to describe their work and to give producers an instant image of where their story is heading and how the audience may read it.

In a pitch situation, you may only have a few minutes to try to interest a producer in your idea. One way of doing this is to describe your story with a 'hook' that can be easily encapsulated and communicated. Defining and refining this 'hook' is a constant challenge to the screenwriter and will be part of your upcoming writing exercises.

Some ideas and subjects are more instantly attractive and communicable than others. Look at the following simple story themes:

- from rags to riches
- jungle boy goes to the big city
- rape victim turned avenger
- the robot who wants to be human
- the peasant who wins the lottery
- the girl who would be queen
- the gangster who chooses between love and money
- the invisible man
- beauty and the beast
- the giant with a heart of gold
- the modern-day Cinderella
- the man and the talking horse
- the android who saves the planet.

These concepts are not only familiar, but are also self-evident. They represent complex ideas that can be simply conveyed in a single phrase. Such familiar story ideas fit in with established genres or types of story that can be found in ancient parables, legends and fables.

Our long history of storytelling means that audiences are familiar with the conventions of various genres. However, audience members are not generally aware of where or how they aquired their historical grasp of such conventions. For instance, you don't need to have read the Bible to be familiar with its stories and character archetypes. You don't need to have read Shakespeare to recognise the basic story of Romeo and Juliet. These story archetypes are such a familiar feature of our culture—deeply ingrained after centuries of story, literature, theatre and song—that they seem to be built in to our awareness.

It would be hard to encapsulate the dramatic impact of a biblical epic such as *Genesis* in a few words, but a high-concept title like *Adam and Eve* helps us get the picture. By recognising how story and character archetypes funtion, you ensure a wider rate of recognition by your audience. People sometimes refer to familiar old stories as being 'trashy' or 'clichéd'. However, we need to consider that one reason a classic becomes a classic is that it has proven its appeal over time.

Such ancient stories may be referred to as 'myths'. Myths are the stories we tell ourselves to explain the mysteries of nature and society, of human behaviour and history. The human urge to repeat these story patterns comes from our need to feel the reassurance and comfort of familiar ideas and legends. This need remains as true today as it was thousands of years ago, when tribal stories were told around a campfire. Screenwriters need to be aware of their role as creators of myth. There is more to telling a story than putting a plot in order. The underlying needs of the audience must also be accounted for.

This means that while certain familiar stories may look relatively simple on the surface, they often have very complex underpinnings, especially in terms of character psychology and their premise. However, these levels of screenplay structure usually work subliminally—that is, beyond the conscious level of audience awareness. The audience usually isn't aware of the way the story's inner complexity is operating. That is the writer's job— to make the story seem easy and natural.

31

In his excellent screenwriting book *The Writer's Journey*, Chris Vogler refers to anthropology and psychology to explain various story forms, characters and types that are a constant feature of both ancient and contemporary storytelling. He points out that these ancient patterns, or archetypes, are so well-proven, so ancient and familiar, that they provide writers with a solid basis for storytelling because they deal with universal themes that reflect humanity in all its variation. In chapter 9, we will examine Vogler's work in some detail, focusing on the mythic character types that can help your story come to life.

Genre defines audience expectations

In cinema, particular story types or genres also follow familiar codes and conventions where repetition is balanced by the introduction of fresh themes and variations.

From the writer's viewpoint, working within a genre or type of story structure means that certain rules or guidelines must be observed. These guidelines relate directly to what an audience needs or expects to see in certain genres.

The conventions of various genres assist the writer to make a connection with the audience. They provide guidelines or signposts that the writer can either observe or depart from. For instance, the audience of a traditional 'Western' movie set during America's 'Wild West' will expect to see the good guys in white hats and the bad guys in black hats, and the gunfight will occur in the main street or in the saloon.

The audience of a traditional science fiction film will expect to be transported to another world in a space ship or to be shown elements of today's science in a future context. While the science fiction hit *Star Wars* describes space travel in a future epoch, it also includes elements of the Western genre. The futuristic setting is balanced by an almost medieval set of mythical elements. The knights, the wizard and the villain are part science fiction, part Western shoot-em-up and part Arthurian legend. This deft crossing of generic types is made more accessible by a solid storyline. As a result, the familiar is given a new context. The good guys (dressed in white) and the bad guys (in black) battle it out on the new frontier—space.

The rules of the genre guide the screenwriter towards all sorts of conventions in character and story development, in setting and location—even in costume. If writing a horror movie, for instance, it is important to assume that the audience's first requirement is to be scared out of their wits. With his recently popular horror series *Scream*, director Wes Craven subverts classic horror conventions by making the monster a peer of the young heroes and setting the horrific attacks not in a gloomy dungeon or haunted house but in a sunny, comfortable middle-class home. He also introduces a strong element of comedy that is an irreverent change from the classic horror genre feature, which is traditionally a dark and dour affair.

The screenwriter needs to work with a clear set of aims that is partly shaped by the genre itself. For instance, if writing in the comedy genre, the aim is to make the audience laugh. In mystery/suspense screenplays, the aim is to create suspense and tension within a high-action framework. Screenwriters need to study genre to ensure that they are observing (or subverting) the key audience requirements of that story type. If these simple audience requirements are not met or addressed, the audience may simply vote with their feet by walking out of the cinema.

Put a twist on familiar themes

Occasionally, a ground-breaking story will smash or lampoon the familiar template of a genre and replace it with a new image or story cycle. This is often the realm of satire and black comedy, perhaps the hardest genres in which to succeed.

A screenplay such as *Pulp Fiction* succeeds in breaking new ground for the gangster genre by placing familiar characters and events in a new context. Writer/director Quentin Tarantino appears to break many classic storytelling rules in this script. For instance, there is no clearly identified protagonist or main character to focus the action. In this fast-moving screenplay, events happen out of chronological order; characters are killed and then brought back on screen in flashbacks and flash-forwards that defy the conventions of classic mainstream cinema.

Despite its unconventional twists, the audience remain tuned-in to the story which is immersed in the traditions of the gangster genre, the boxing drama and the *noir* thriller. So, while the story takes big risks in some areas, it generally sticks closely to a quite traditional core.

Look at the characters in *Pulp Fiction*—tough-guy hitmen, the femme fatale and the boxer are all familiar figures who anchor the audience in what may otherwise seem like a chaotic or confusing plot. In this case, the familiar, genre-based characters and themes add solidity to the potentially confusing ordering of events.

In a similar way, a screenplay such as *Thelma & Louise* challenges the usual cinematic treatment of both romance and gender. The story is anchored firmly within two genres—the Western, and the road-movie or buddy-picture. The solid structures of these genres allow the writer, Callie Khouri, to take risks with themes and subject matter (violent and vengeful rape victims, female outlaws) that may otherwise be simply too challenging or 'out there' for the audience. Much of the irony of this female road-movie derives from its setting—fair and square within the mythic territory of the cowboy-centred Western.

This means that while a story may incorporate challenging or up-to-the-minute techniques or subject matter, it may be strengthened by the inclusion of elements that are familiar to the audience. Mythic archetypes of character, location and plot can help an audience feel at home with story material that may otherwise look too risky or innovative.

The producer's big questions: Who cares? and So what?

To connect with an audience and their dreams, the writer needs to develop material within a specific genre that actually has something definite to say to a specific audience. To check whether the writer has thought about all this, producers may ask three key questions of the nervous writer at their first meeting:

- Who cares?
- So what?
- What is your story *really* about?

These questions sound simple, but they are usually the hardest questions to answer. They force the writer to consider what they are really trying to examine or express in the film script. They concern the fundamental premise or reason behind the story. If a writer cannot answer these questions they are in trouble, as this will suggest that they haven't gone beneath the surface level of their work to consider the underlying levels of the story.

Let's say that William Shakespeare pitches the story of *Romeo and Juliet* to a movie producer. 'It's a romantic tragi-comedy where boy gets girl, boy loses girl and then both of them die.'

'Hmm,' says the producer. 'This sounds promising; we like the romance, but it could be a little gloomy. So tell me,' the producer asks, cutting to the core issue, 'Who cares?'

If Shakespeare has done his job and thought about the audience, he can point out that the poetic yearnings of young lovers provide a universal theme that many may relate to. 'So what?' says the producer. 'I have a dozen romances on my desk here. What makes this one so special?' Shakespeare points out that *Romeo and Juliet* is no ordinary romance. It is enriched by themes involving warring families, blood feuds, and miscommunication that can lead to terrible consequences. It is also the story of a love that knows no bounds.

Shakespeare begins to unpack the layers of his story: 'Juliet and Romeo come from warring families. The twist is that their friends and loved ones are responsible for setting them on a path of lies and subterfuge. This in turn leads to miscommunication, which can only end in tragedy. The young lovers are naive; they must hide their love from the world and, as a result, end up betraying themselves and each other. It's a story with heart!'

'Yes, interesting,' admits the producer. 'But what is your story *really* about?' Now, Shakespeare understands that the producer is looking for a story that has some substance; a story with subtext; a story that goes deeper than the surface levels to reveal the moral, philosophical and cultural intrigues of the day. 'It's *really* about the naivety of youth and the corruption of age. It's about social hierarchies and family conflict affecting the inner life of individuals. It's really about young love and idealism being destroyed by stifling social conventions and feuds within the oligarchies of neo-industrial Italy. At the same time it's about youth and gullibility . . . a story full of irony and savage social critique. It's a timely and relevant story!'

Shakespeare then pulls out a newspaper article about two lovers committing a double suicide only last week in a Hong Kong hotel. 'See?' he says. 'This story is as relevant today as it was last year and will be twenty years from now. It's as relevant in China as it is in Europe. It's a universal story with plenty of classic audience appeal!'

At this point, the producer may be convinced that this writer has really thought about his material on a multitude of levels and researched his characters well. *Romeo and Juliet* puts a fresh, contemporary twist on a classic story. This makes it a good bet from an audience point of view. The producer buys it.

The producer will nearly always ask the writer to make changes to their script before committing to the project. So the writer must be flexible and prepared to change elements of their story in line with a producer's needs. 'Maybe Juliet could be a chambermaid instead of a princess?' the producer suggests. Shakespeare knows this is a bad idea, but he keeps his laughter in check. Writers need great skills in diplomacy and persuasion to handle this aspect of their job. As a token of his flexibility and goodwill, Shakespeare may offer to change another aspect of the story but may fight to leave the central mechanism in place. Until they are famous and well-respected, young writers should understand that it's best not to be too stubborn nor to bite the hand that feeds them.

EXERCISE 1

Creating your screenplay folio

Dedicate a special notebook to your screenplay project. Use this folio to relax into any kind of prose style you like—notes, essay form, poetry, whatever. The idea is to get your creative juices flowing and to take on a 'god-like' perspective where you are in control of every aspect of your protagonist's world—both inner and outer.

In this folio, you will compile notes about your protagonist and their life story. You will include notes on other key characters—family, lovers, antagonists—who may become your key support roles.

First make some notes on your own hopes as a writer. Try to understand your own strengths, weaknesses and motives for writing. Describe how these may enable you to make a better exploration of your screen world, and consider how they may equip you with more choices in terms of the field or subject matter that excites you. How can you work with your perceived strengths and weaknesses? Consider also your ambitions as a storyteller for your 'tribe', culture or community.

Ask yourself the following questions:

- What kind of locations and characters do you want to write about?
- Is there a particular set of human problems that you want to question or dramatise with this work?
- What aspects of human behaviour and culture would you like to examine in your screenplay?
- What is motivating you as a writer? Is there a fire in your belly?
- Is there something about the world that angers you and that you want to communicate to others?
- Is there some inner pain, joy, frustration or realisation that you need to communicate?

- What genre or type of film do you need to write?
- Is there a point, a theme, a premise or some issue in particular that may drive your work?

Think about your potential audience.

- Who are they?
- What would you like to give them in the way of insights or ideas?
- What will draw them to your work?

Begin to explore the story material that you may develop further in your folio.

- Make a list of people, events and locations that interest you.
- Make a list of stories that involve these characters, themes and events. Write a list of sketch stories that involve your characters, themes and events.
- Begin to outline one or two particular favourites, taking note of who the main protagonist may be in each one.

2

Know the rules before you break them

Chapter objectives
To understand
the special codes
of a screenplay
document; to
identify the four
fundamental
building blocks of
good story structure
and define the
function of each;
to examine the
elements that create
character psychol-
ogy; and to explore
how a protagonist
with a motive can
lead the writer to a
solid plot.

In the previous chapter, you reflected on your role as a storyteller. You also considered the kind of subjects and themes that matter to you. In this chapter, we will identify the fundamental structures of the writer's craft. These include four interlocking elements that are the structural backbone of any story: the protagonist, dramatic problem, plot and premise.

Our goal is to help you refine your story ideas and to provide technical guidance on how to write them in screenplay form. First, we will introduce a few foundation techniques. Once you understand how these work, you can play with them creatively.

We have established that it isn't difficult to generate story ideas. The task here, however, goes far beyond that. We will now ask you to undertake the disciplined work of a professional writer: to commit to a story and then execute it. Your challenge is to understand the screenplay document as a special literary form with a unique set of technical requirements.

In order to write a successful screenplay, you must also get to know your protagonist by creating a profile or 'backstory' for them as if they were a real person, complete with complex psychology and motivations.

The screenplay is a coded document

A good screenplay must represent the technical needs of the producer and crew while at the same time accommodating and representing the imaginative needs of the audience. The writer needs to meet both of these requirements in order to attract a producer who will be prepared to pay for the production.

In general, the structure of a screenplay must be sturdy enough to support the characters and the plot. It must also support the requirements of the producer and other industry professionals who will make many concrete business decisions based on the document. The screenwriter must account for all of this, as well as for the audience requirements that help to shape any film. The writer must ensure that the story relates to the audience's expectations and needs: Does it make sense? Is it appealing, timely and exciting? Does it fit within a certain genre, or does it subvert that genre? Does it tell us something we didn't already know or put a twist on a classic theme?

While a screenplay is a relatively short document, it is a complex one. There are multiple levels or dimensions to this interesting literary structure. Many aspects of the screenplay are concrete and tangible, such as the instructions regarding costume, dialogue, action and location. These technical and artistic requirements are discussed in detail in chapters 7 and 8. Other more subtle aspects of the screenplay document relate to its function within the film industry. As well as being an artistic statement, the script will imply technical and business decisions to do with investment, audience and distribution.

In general, story structure must represent the world and the characters of the writer's imagination in a way that makes sense to a potential producer, director, cast and crew. These people are the first line of readers for a screenplay. The actual film audience will never read the script; they only view the film object itself, which is an interpretation or a 'materialisation' of the writer's conception.

Just as an architect or engineer must understand the rules of construction, screenwriters need a few basic rules to ensure that they meet the multiple requirements of a strong story structure. The journey from concept to finished film product is a long and expensive one and requires careful technical and artistic adjustments along the way.

Understanding the screenplay document

Before we move on to a very concrete discussion of the screenplay's forms and functions, it is worth clarifying its exact function. New screenwriters often confuse the screenplay with other forms of literature and write elaborate stage directions that are like passages in a novel or short story. This error in logic will be addressed in upcoming chapters. For now, let's consider that the screenplay definitely is not a form of novel. Nor is it a short story. The screenplay is perhaps more akin to the architect's blueprint or the symphonic score than it is to the novel. In any case, it is both a pure literary and craft form that obeys a distinct set of rules.

We have seen that the script must be timely—that is, it must be relevant to the culture of the day. The story must be believable and appealing, be peopled with fully realised characters, be animated by colourful action and locations, and be driven by an interesting and coherent plot.

To achieve all of this, the screenwriter must produce a coded set of instructions that has a highly specific technical function. The screenplay is a specially coded document that is unlike any other kind of story text. The screenwriter drafts the screenplay as a kind of conceptual 'map' of an imaginary 'world'.

The screenplay is the blueprint of the film's story world—of the action and dialogue. The writer should not be confused about what is 'the main event'. The screenplay is not the finished product; it is a highly coded and detailed instruction manual for the further creation of the finished product—the film. From an audience's viewpoint, the *film* is the main event. From the writer's viewpoint, the screenplay is the seminal phase in the creation of this event and it is the writer's role to envisage both.

Now, it is true that screenplays can be written with all the precision and irony of Haiku poetry, with all the majesty of epic theatre, with passion, romance and razor-sharp insight. However, unlike a novel, an essay or a poem, which are read directly by a public audience or readership, the screenplay isn't written to be judged as an artistic text in itself. The screenwriter is not appealing directly to the audience with their text. They must first pass muster with a crew and cast of industry craftspeople—the producer, director, technical crew and actors who then follow the writer's instructions and specifications to construct an entire imaginary realm for the screen.

The screenplay isn't written to amuse or delight the reader with poetry or prose; it is written to bring the writer's story world to life by instructing a team of professionals about the technical requirements of the onscreen storytelling project.

We might compare the screenplay to the symphonic score, which is a set of instructions for a number of instruments or voices. Like the symphonic score, the screenplay is not written specifically for the audience at 'the event'. Like musical notation, the screenplay is a set of coded instructions for a group of crafts-people and performers. They will use the document to envisage and rehearse a number of 'set pieces' or movements—to create, enact and perform the 'events' using very specific timing.

We might also compare the screenplay to the architect's designs for a grand building. Like the architect's blueprint, the screenplay is a preparatory document that instructs a team of professionals in the creation of a complex, multi-dimensional structure or 'object'. The architect must prepare a set of blueprints that 'make sense'. The codes and formats of this design, the measurements and the calculations that are represented in the drawings and figures, must all add up to the creation of a safe and sturdy structure that is appealing to the eye and will survive the ravages of time.

It sounds simplistic and obvious to remind writers that what they are describing on paper may eventually exist in a real dimension, inside a studio or on location, where real actors and props will be put to use to realise the vision that is created on paper. The screenplay represents one of the most abstract levels of human thought. It is a highly coded written form that carries an enormous wealth of symbolic content, as well as purely technical information. The script conveys information about images and sounds. It describes what the audience will see and hear, what the actors will do and say. For those reading 'between the lines', the screenplay also conveys information about what it all 'means' on a conceptual level, about the writer's point of view, and about issues and ideas, themes, attitudes and human problems.

In this way, the screenplay is really a kind of alchemical formula; it is an instruction manual for the conjuring of human action and behaviour that a team of performers and craftspeople will make 'real' using the document as their guide. Thus the screenplay allows the creation of a parallel universe where creatures of the writer's inner vision are given artificial life and enabled to strut upon the stage of our collective imagination.

In order to achieve their vision, the screenwriter must first compete with other writers looking for favour. They must then communicate across several audiences who will inevitably be highly critical of the endeavour. As teams of other creative people—the director, composer, actors and crew—add their contributions and critiques, the original vision of the screenwriter may become diluted. The screenplay may be changed or even abandoned by the cast and crew it was intended for.

In order to protect or guarantee the strength of their artistic vision, the writer needs to understand where they can have the most creative control over that vision. They need to understand the specific contours of the screenplay form. This allows them to protect the unity and integrity of their work by creating a structured document that will withstand the scrutiny of many other interested parties.

The maxim 'less is more' applies to screenwriting in the same way that it applies to the manufacture of high-precision Swiss watches or microchip circuitry. With a mere 120 or so pages to play with, the screenwriter is required to make an almost surgical use of language. The task is to say as much as possible about a character or situation in as few words as possible. The writer must deal with strict limitations on word and page numbers.

For example, let's say that you are editing your first-draft screenplay down from 200 to 100 pages. You notice that in some important stage directions you describe a tree as a 'gigantic mass of waving branches, dipping and swaying like a scarecrow in the wind'. You may decide to cut the 'purple prose' and just say 'tree'. This cuts a line and thirteen unnecessary words from your script; an editorial triumph.

However, if the image of the scarecrow is crucial to your set-up and themes, then make a calculated decision to focus on this image or word in a stage direction. You can still save ten words by changing the description to 'scarecrow-like tree', which now becomes a project for the art department to consider. By including the word 'scarecrow', the writer is instructing the crew that a specific type of tree should be used for the scene. If this descriptor is not crucial to the action or the mood, chances are it will be cut in the final script edit, when the writer is inevitably (and often frantically) looking for ways to reduce clutter and wordage.

Knowing they are always under pressure to 'cut, cut, cut!', a good screenwriter will justify each word as part of a larger code that is both poetic and technical. They understand that the screenplay isn't an art form in itself. Rather, it represents a seminal phase in a further process that leads to the creation of a more complex art form—the film. The screenplay provides coded instructions for the creation of a complex artistic event or 'object' that will take place after the screenwriter has finished their phase of the creative process. Within this code, every word is a beat in the overall scheme. Every word must count.

The four Ps

We now move to screenwriting 'nuts and bolts'. Because the screenplay includes so many aspects of narrative—character, locations, chronology (or timing) and action—story structure is often the most complex aspect of the screenplay to organise. Let's begin there.

A good screenplay includes four main structures. Let's call them the four Ps:

- the protagonist
- the dramatic problem
- the plot
- the premise.

Now let's define them briefly.

The protagonist

This ancient theatrical term refers to the lead character who is defined by five main features:

- their physical and psychological nature—their inner and outer worlds
- their history—things that occurred before the story begins
- their immediate dramatic problem—the key dilemma that helps to shape the plot in the 'here and now' of screen-time

- their character arc or journey, which describes how and why they end up in a different state from where they began
- the premise or viewpoint of the writer.

During the course of the plot, the audience needs to like— preferably even 'love'—the protagonist in order to relate to their problem and thus stay committed to the story.

According to the Greek philosopher, Aristotle, who wrote on poetry and theatre in 330 BC, in good drama, a complex process of identification occurs between the audience and the protagonist such that the audience imaginatively becomes one with the protagonist. The audience members imagine themselves as the hero or heroine of the story, identify with their problems and passions and gain a tremendous emotional release, or catharsis, at the end of a successfully resolved story.

To help this process along, the writer must create a fully realised, sympathetic protagonist; a character who hits the screen complete with a rich 'backstory', or history, plus a psychological profile that mirrors our own. The writer must create a protagonist whose psychology or 'inner' world is quite clearly mapped out. This means the writer must consider the protagonist's needs, fears, goals, problems, passions, dreams and motives in order that we understand fully their actions on screen.

The central dramatic problem

The writer creates a special story mechanism to lure an audience into the story. This is known as the central dramatic problem. The writer endows the protagonist with this problem in order to keep the plot moving. The problem is usually comprised of an organised set of obstacles or dilemmas for the protagonist to solve.

Let's say that the readers of the screenplay represent the interests of both the producer and the audience. If these two groups can relate to the central dramatic problem, they are more likely to 'buy' the story. The producer will only be interested in paying for a production that will appeal to the concerns of a wide audience. Producers know that an audience will 'buy' a story if they can empathise with the protagonist and their problems.

The central dramatic problem drives the plot by providing complications and obstacles for the protagonist to deal with. It is crucial that this problem be resolved in a way that is satisfying to the audience, as this is the essence of their cathartic release or pleasure in the story.

The plot

The plot usually follows the protagonist's attempts to solve the complications arising from the central dramatic problem. The plot also relates to the organisation of events, action and dialogue within the time frame or chronology of the overall story. The audience watches the plot closely to pick up clues relating to the emotional and physical journey or character arc of the protagonist. This journey is the central spine of the screenplay and is usually described in terms of three acts that relate to the beginning, middle and end of the story.

The writer's first priority is to create a plot that is 'tight' and coherent. If the story is interrupted by 'gaps' and 'holes' that don't make sense, the illusion of the story is shattered and the general effect is one of audience confusion and disappointment.

Producers sometimes assert that the plot is what sells a film, not the talent, the art direction or the locations. Other producers will tell you that 'the talent', or the movie stars are the ingredients that sell a script, no matter what the story is like.

Until you have the ability to 'attach' big-name actors to your script, your plot is the main selling point. The organisation of the story is therefore a primary concern of the writer and of the producer who evaluates the screenplay. Rather than organising your screenplay around events alone, it is crucial to consider the protagonist, their psychology and their main problem as important elements that may help you to formulate the plot.

The premise

The premise is the writer's secret weapon, their 'ace in the hole'. This central concept often comes out of the moral, philosophical, spiritual or intellectual idea that drives the writer to write in the first place. It is an abstract idea that the writer must struggle to make concrete, using the structural means at their disposal.

The premise is the overall concept that governs the story. It is the central statement or theme that the writer expresses through the unfolding of character and plot. A writer with a strong attitude or viewpoint to communicate has the power to move an audience. To achieve this, the writer must give the characters in the story a sense of conviction, whether it be expressed as anger or humour. There must also be a strong emotion, passion or idea at the centre of a story.

A good writer constructs the plot, the protagonist and their dramatic problem as vehicles for the film's premise or viewpoint. However, the audience isn't usually aware of the writer's premise, which is an invisible support that works from deep within the structure. The premise is the central, most important theme. Strong professional writers are often able to articulate their premise before embarking on their first draft. Other writers use the first draft as a kind of rough experiment in order to identify and articulate the central theme. The premise is often the most obscure or elusive story element to identify among the other themes, ideas and images that can jostle for attention in the writer's busy mind. The sooner the writer identifies their premise, the stronger the work will be.

The premise is also the most difficult theoretical element to discuss, as it represents one of the most ethereal aspects of the writing. The writer must have the patience or the focus to identify a premise in their work. The premise is often invisible to the audience. Rather than being stated baldly or even acted out, the premise is usually part of the 'smoke and mirrors' of the underlying story structure. It works at a subliminal or subconscious level

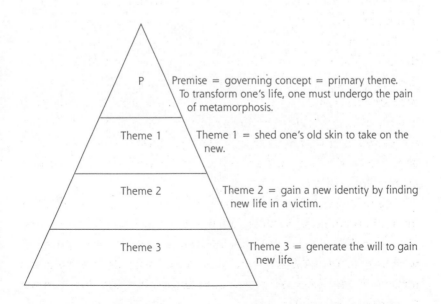

Figure 2.1   The Silence of the Lambs

to help convey a strong idea that goes beyond concrete action into the realm of feeling or mood.

Think of your premise as the central, most important theme. It's an idea which will be repeated again and again in different ways throughout the script (see figure 2.1).

Strong stories are organised around a well-organised set of themes which help to cement the premise and to imbue the story and characters with flavour or attitude. For example, in the Oscar-winning *The Silence of the Lambs*, one of the central themes was metamorphosis. This theme was present in the journey of the protagonist, Clarice Starling, as she undergoes her initiation from a trainee FBI officer to an active officer in the field. The metamorphosis theme is also embodied in the monstrous villain who steals the skin of his victims in order to make a body suit that will transform him into the creature of his dreams. The same theme is present in the image of the butterfly, a creature that transforms or metamorphoses and which recurs as a visual motif throughout the story. It is also present in the image of the young FBI cadet taking on the responsibility of being a fully fledged officer.

The audience of *The Silence of the Lambs* may not really 'see' the writer's premise on a conscious level. However, on close examination of the script, it seems clear that the writer includes evidence for his premise in every scene. According to one reading, the story seems to prove the point that in order to transform oneself and gain a new life, a creature must shed their former 'skin' and undergo the pain of metamorphosis. In another reading, the premise may concern something more specific about the nature of evil: the killer is seeking a new skin, a new identity, through the deaths of his victims. The heroine also finds a new identity—as an FBI officer—having undergone her ordeal.

It isn't always possible to isolate and identify a single premise for a story. That is often the secret realm of the writer. However, it is imperative that when writing your own story, you organise your themes around the guiding principle of a central or governing concept that can give shape and consistency to the work.

It takes some experience to get a total grip on how a premise operates, so be patient. The exercises in this book will guide you in your thinking. In general, the premise is like a private guideline that helps the writer to shape every scene. It helps them stay on track, organising the plot, the protagonist and the dramatic problem according to a clear vision or definite viewpoint.

When a producer asks you, 'who cares?', you should have a clearly thought-out premise on which to base your answer. The producer of *The Silence of the Lambs* may have even asked the screenwriter, 'So who cares about a serial killer with a butterfly fixation?' And the writer probably replied, 'Anyone who has ever been desperate to transform their own life. Metamorphosis from monster to beauty always involves pain and struggle.' Now, *that's* a premise worth looking at.

Some writers search for a premise before beginning their story. Others find it as they work their way through. The writer's challenge is to find the right plot to help explain or understand events that are essential to their concerns and passions. One purpose for all this is to entertain the audience; another is to understand what ethical, philosophical or moral points can be made about the events that take place. This makes for intelligent writing as opposed to light-weight junk.

Don't assume that intelligent writing is only for serious or 'heavy' drama. The responsibility to communicate organised ideas is equally as pressing in comedy as it is in drama. Some of the funniest comedies have the most 'loaded' premises. Consider, for instance, Stanley Kubrick's *Dr Strangelove*. This hilarious black comedy delivers enormous wisdom about the follies of nuclear war. It packages some extremely complex political and ethical ideas in a comedic plot that has the audience helpless with laughter. In this way, Kubrick manages to deliver a deadly serious message about war. He 'sugar coats' his message in a framework of parody, satire and slapstick. Charlie Chaplin's films *Limelight* and *The Great Dictator* achieve a similar effect, using a clownish protagonist to represent highly contentious ideas about politics and the society of the time.

How the four Ps interlock

The four Ps are interlocked in a seamless whole that may be thought of as the hidden framework or structure of the story. This invisible structure is like a house of cards: if one of these elements—protagonist, problem, plot, premise—isn't in order, the rest of the structure will collapse. For instance, the writer can never really consider the protagonist without also considering their dramatic problem. This dramatic problem in turn will affect the logic of the plot, which describes the beginning, middle and end phases of the protagonist's struggle.

Finally, each of these structures is basically determined by the premise, which provides the writer with a sense of the 'big picture'—the overall philosophy, idea or logic that guides the story.

EXERCISE 2

The log book

Before we move forward with screenwriting work, we will focus on the importance of reading other screenplays. As a way of reinforcing your understanding of screenwriting technique, it is crucial that you read as much high quality screenplay material as you can. You need to keep track of your reading by keeping a log book of scripts you've read.

New writers argue that watching a lot of movies is the best way to develop as a screenwriter, but they are actually confusing two very different processes and media: one on the screen and one on the page.

Watching a movie doesn't offer any insight into the way stage directions, dialogue, pacing and characterisation are handled from the writer's viewpoint. Reading the screenplay and comparing it to the film is a great way of working, but don't be fooled into thinking that watching the film alone will give any insight into how a good screenplay is written.

Of course, it helps to be inspired by excellent films, but your task as a writer is to actively engage with a very particular written medium that exists on a different plane to the movie itself. Screenwriting is first about putting words on to a page. Only then will the director be able to project what you have imagined on to the screen.

Read as many screenplays as you can find and take notes in your log book on their structure, observing the structural elements that are described in the following chapters. These include the key turning points, characterisation and so on. Observe how each of the scripts you read handles the three-act structure and use this as a template or model by which to understand the screenplay material you are writing yourself.

Screenplays are best read in the standard industry format so that you get a sense of the layout and length of dialogue and stage directions. Industry-format scripts can be purchased at specialist theatrical bookstores and are often quite costly. Local libraries also keep screenplays but often in a book format that is different from the industry format. Film industry organisations, government authorities and film clubs often have libraries from where it is possible to borrow screenplays.

It is also possible to download scripts off the Internet, but take care to locate authorised versions. Some sites employ amateur writers to transcribe dialogue from the filmed versions and print this up as a screenplay. These pirated scripts are to be avoided as they don't represent the work of the original screenwriter.

3

The psychology of the protagonist

To explore how the central dramatic problem comes out of character psychology.

We have discussed the role of the four Ps—the protagonist, dramatic problem, plot and premise. These are the fundamental structures that will support your screenplay.

- The protagonist is the lead character defined by their back-story, motives, dilemmas, needs and fears.
- The dramatic problem consists of an organised set of obstacles or dilemmas for the protagonist to solve.
- The plot relates to the organisation of events, actions and dialogue within the time frame of the story.
- The premise is the overall concept that governs the story.

Now let's focus on the role of the protagonist as the key to each of the other structural components of your screenplay.

The protagonist is the central figure in your screenplay—the most fully realised onscreen character who attracts audience attention in most scenes.

In order to organise your ideas for a story, start writing a biography of your protagonist. This will enable you to really get to know this character as if they were an old friend or—even more intimately—your child; after all, this key character is your total creation. To achieve this, the writer must summon all their technical and artistic skills in order to portray their protagonist in great detail, endowing them with distinctive and individual qualities, actions, problems and behaviour.

As a screenwriter, you are essentially creating a 'world' from the ground up. Part of your job is to plan and design every single element of the protagonist's environment that will eventually appear on screen. These elements include:

- the environment and locations
- the characters and events
- the ideas, passions and ethics that govern the characters and their actions.

Reflect for a moment and then make notes on films that are memorable in regard to these points.

Three acts: The beginning, middle and end

If we look at both ancient and contemporary forms of dramatic storytelling—ancient myths, legends, folk tales, holy books and plays; novels, comic books, opera and film—it is easy to identify key patterns or formulas in the structure of plot.

Classic cinema structure is based on the ancient European tradition of a simple, linear narrative where three acts represent the beginning, middle and end of the protagonist's story. This basic narrative formula was as relevant to the writers of the Bible as it is to the screenwriters of tomorrow.

Your protagonist moves forward on the journey that is the main narrative line or thread of their story. Along the way, they undergo various changes and adventures—both physical and psychological—according to the plot.

Marking out the protagonist's journey

In act one, the writer's main job is to set up the basic world of the story and to establish or observe the rules that govern that world. The writer establishes the main character or protagonist, whom we meet in their 'normal' world or environment. The writer then creates a disturbance in that world as the protagonist's 'normal' situation is upturned. This disturbance produces a conflict and a central dramatic problem for the protagonist.

In act two, the writer follows through on the act one set-up. A struggle ensues as the protagonist's dramatic problem is further complicated. This is achieved using technical plot devices such as obstacles, reversals and barriers that create conflict between the characters.

Finally, in act three, the writer builds the plot towards a climax by putting the protagonist into a final conflict with the key support roles. The problem is then set right, or partly set right. The central dramatic problem must be resolved in the end. This leads to the denouement or resolution, which indicates how the protagonist finally deals with their central problem. The resolution also suggests the future direction for the protagonist; the direction the story will take after the curtain has come down.

Within this classic three-act plot structure, the protagonist must be dynamic—that is, they must change during the course of the story so that they end up in a different physical, emotional or spiritual state from where they began. This kind of dramatic movement or change is usually described as the protagonist's arc or journey.

The changes undergone by the protagonist may be physical or psychological, or both. For instance, your protagonist may end up in a different house with a new partner and with a new outlook on life; thus, the physical change may reflect changes that have occurred in the inner, psychological realm. Or they may stay in the same house with the same partner but have a new outlook, thus indicating that inner or psychological change can transcend material things.

Rules governing the protagonist

There are a few simple rules to remember regarding the protagonist.

The protagonist is the focus

In classic drama, the protagonist must be the primary, proactive agent for change. In the course of their trials, problems and challenges, they cannot be saved by someone else or let off the hook by some magical solution without first having proved their grit and their humanity to the audience. This sense of the quest, the struggle or the journey is what audiences (without necessarily realising it) need to identify with. In most genres, you need to focus on a single protagonist to achieve this.

There needs to be just one protagonist

The classic dramatic form is focused around a single protagonist. In some genres, such as the buddy-picture or the screwball comedy, there may be two protagonists who function as flipsides of the same coin. In recent dramas of the kind pioneered by Robert Altman and Quentin Tarantino, there is often a large ensemble cast where three, or even four, characters may be given equal weight.

We suggest that, for now, you focus on a single character in the classic form. It's hard enough to develop a single character journey without worrying about balancing the demands of extra roles. Later chapters will examine more complex structural options.

For now be careful not to create two main characters. Having more than one main character may weaken the plot by distracting the audience from the main conflict or problem. An antagonist or a love interest is technically a support role for the protagonist. Support roles aren't as central as the protagonist and, rather than take up too much time, should function mainly to tell us something about the protagonist.

The protagonist proves your premise

Remember to use the protagonist as a vehicle for your premise. What is the larger theme or idea you are trying to express with your screenplay? The journey of the protagonist must help you to prove or articulate your central premise and themes.

Character motivation leads into the central dramatic problem

By definition, conflict is the stuff of drama and an effective protagonist is largely defined by their response to a central problem or dilemma. Just as we often don't really know our friends until we see them under pressure, the protagonist reveals their true self when dealing with challenging tasks and problems. When the writer provides the protagonist with a clear motivating factor, their problems are made more apparent and painful.

When the writer considers the protagonist's motivation for change, this often leads to the formulation of the character's central dramatic problem. By creating a gripping dramatic problem for the protagonist to solve, the writer reveals the character's psychology and can direct the action accordingly.

The central dramatic problem usually sets the agenda for action in the feature film. This problem keeps the protagonist active and on their toes, moving forward to face the challenges that confront them. Without a clear motive, it is easy for the protagonist to lose focus and for the story to get bogged down.

The writer uses the dramatic problem to keep the audience on the edge of their seats in a state of suspense. Ideally, the audience should always be wondering, 'If he's not careful, a guy with this motivation could get into trouble. How will the protagonist deal with this problem now? What will happen next?'

The central problem drives both the protagonist and the plot forward by providing a reason and a context for the action. Several clear-cut techniques can help you to work out how this might take place. An understanding of psychological motivation and of the character's history or backstory is central to this aspect of the screenwriter's craft.

Character backstory

In order to appear fully 'fleshed-out', the protagonist must have a history, or backstory, which helps to explain or colour their current actions onscreen. Even though you may end up writing only about two weeks in the life of this person, you need to give them extra dimension by providing them with a total history that describes what occurred in the character's 'life' before the action begins onscreen.

In order to understand your protagonist and their motives, it is important to consider not only their entire lifetime but also:

- the key events that will influence the unfolding of your story
- events and scenes that occur in the past, present and future of onscreen story time
- the human needs common to us all—survival, bonding, success and self-esteem, health and so on
- their small personal preferences and details—where they would go for lunch, where they went to school, their likes and dislikes, where their parents are from.

Remember that conflict is the essence of all story types, whether it be comedy or drama. The conflict or tension between the protagonist and the support roles will add more weight to the central problem. Consider how conflict may be structured into your story by focusing on the various relations between:

- the protagonist and other characters
- different realms or domains of the protagonist's outer environment
- different ideas, goals or motives that motivate the protagonist (and the writer!).

Even though this extensive written research and preparation may not be present in the script, it is essential background material for the generation of your screenplay.

The screenplay is a deceptively slim document. The pages of crucial screenplay material that a producer or director does *not* see are the pages of notes, stories, dialogue and research that a writer creates in the early stages of the screenplay drafting process.

The committed writer understands the alchemy of creation; that ideas and images can only be called 'art' when they are externalised, articulated and committed to a medium that others can see, recognise and appreciate.

It makes sense, then, that when writing for the screen, the best writers prepare a weighty folio of ideas, sketches, stories and biographies that helps them to conjure or 'create' the world of their story. They write down where their protagonist would go for lunch, why they dropped out of school or who they had a crush on as a teenager, who their best friends are. Such information is the essential background on characters that writers refer to when making decisions about actions and events. It's all part of the basic 'material', the basic clay, out of which the writer constructs the finished screenplay. This is the stuff of your screenwriting folio.

In many instances, a character's backstory will emerge directly in the narrative. Important details about a character's past will inform the audience of where they are coming from. They can also drive the plot by providing clues about the action.

For example, in *Basic Instinct*, we learn that Detective Nick Curran (known as 'Shooter') is simultaneously drawn to guns and repelled by the consequences of their use. He is a guy who lives on the edge of extreme danger. Nick must investigate the backstory, or history, of several of the support characters in order to investigate a murder. In this way the audience learns about action that occurred before the curtain rises on the drama.

In *Basic Instinct*, the backstory of the support characters is conveyed in a police history or record for each suspect. When Nick meets a woman whose backstory is similar to his own, he is attracted to her. This backstory provides Nick (and the audience) with information needed to solve a crime in the present. In this way, the history of the characters helps to explain the action in the present. It also helps the audience to put together the clues that solve a mystery.

In *Thelma & Louise*, we meet two women on the cusp of middle age who need to redefine their relationships with men. Thelma is a dissatisfied housewife who leaves her husband and goes all out for a new freedom. Louise is a waitress whose shadowy past contributes to her trouble with the law. We catch many glimpses of Louise's backstory. There are suggestions in the dialogue that she may have been raped and then committed a felony in Texas years before. This information helps to explain why she wants to avoid driving through Texas at all costs. It also helps to explain why she used a gun in the first place to defend her friend from a rapist.

In *Breakfast at Tiffany's*, we learn that while Holly Golightly may act like an urban princess, she actually comes from a 'white trash' background. Through old photos and dialogue, we learn that she comes from a poor, hillbilly background and was married as a young girl. This information helps to explain Holly's need to escape poverty and to cultivate her persona as the city sophisticate. The tension between her backstory and her 'present' produces much of the drama in this exciting romance.

While all the colourful details of the character's past, or 'off-screen' life, may not actually be referred to directly in the screenplay, such details help the writer to get a 'feel' for the character. Heightened knowledge of these details also helps them to make decisions about what characters would or wouldn't do or say in response to situations and events.

Writing a screenplay is a little like carving a figure from a piece of stone. If we were to ask Michelangelo, he would tell us that a big block of stone is often required to create a small sculpture.

The artist must cut away huge chunks of material in order to reveal the finished piece. Screenwriting includes a similar process of creation, elimination, selection and polishing. It is crucial for the writer to generate a large body of material from which key elements can be selected for polishing as part of the onscreen world. This is why your screenwriting folio is such an important tool.

Character motivation

According to Aristotle, the writer of a character on stage must reveal a moral purpose. By showing the audience what kind of things a person chooses or avoids, the writer reveals the inner emotions, passions and fears that are driving that character to action. These days we call this the motivation of a character—the inner psychological state that pushes them into action.

In considering their backstory, psychology and motivation, ask yourself:

- What are the protagonist's main values, attitudes and beliefs?
- What are the protagonist's main desires, needs and goals?
- What are the protagonist's main fears, vanities, delusions and foibles?

Answering these questions in some depth will endow your protagonist with a clearly defined goal or aim. For instance, if their goal is to be a champion athlete, give the character a focus by setting them a concrete aim—they want to win a gold medal at the Olympic Games.

It also helps to study the character's psychology in some depth. If you understand the difference between what a character *wants* and what they really *need*, it allows you to point out their delusions and foibles. For instance, a character may *want* to win an

Olympic medal, but the writer lets the audience know that what that character really *needs* may be true love or fatherly approval. Consider how our human tendency to confuse our wants with our needs can lead to conflict and problems.

The realms of the protagonist

In this section we focus on two realms of the protagonist:

- their outer world—the realm of action
- their inner world—the realm of psychology.

The external realm represents the tangible, outer 'real' world of the protagonist. The internal realm represents their inner, psychological or imaginative world. The protagonist's problem is often the result of—and the plot will be driven by—a clash between these two worlds.

It is up to the writer to show how events and action in the external realm are reflected and motivated by the conflict in the protagonist's inner realm. The writer may then shape the protagonist's journey to prove or illustrate how action affects psychology, and vice versa.

External conflict	Internal conflict
Lost job	Inability to focus
Unfaithful lover	Fear of betrayal
Sick child	Loss of religious faith
Use of drugs	Lack of self-confidence

When considering the kind of protagonist you wish to create, think hard about the conflicts that occur during their journey over three acts. How can you best dramatise 'inner' turmoil using imagery and locations in the 'outer' world?

Conflict as the basic building block of drama

Your protagonist will be dealing with a clearly identified set of problems and conflicts:

- Their responses will be shaped by their 'inner' world, or the psychology you equip them with.
- To a lesser extent, their responses will be shaped by the 'outer' world, as well as by the actions of other key characters.
- Their responses will be shaped by their history or backstory.

For instance, if your protagonist is obsessed with money, where might they work or live? If they are 'looking for love in all the wrong places', where might we find them? At a nightclub? Having tennis lessons? If your protagonist is torn between their love of worldly luxury and their love of nature, where might you set the crucial scenes that exemplify this clash? A casino? A surf beach?

The external 'world' of the protagonist can help you to structure all kinds of conflict within your plot. For instance, consider some of the inner problems that arise when the (outer) world of work collides with the (inner) demands of the romantic realm. This clash of worlds is the good, basic stuff of a wide range of comedy and drama genres.

Consider the following classic pairs and observe how the genre, or type of story, can affect the writer's choice of realms in which the action may take place:

- the world of career versus the world of romance (romantic drama/comedy; e.g. *Working Girl*)
- the world of crime versus the world of family (gangster genre, e.g. *The Godfather*)
- the world of war versus the world of peace (war movies and adventure, e.g. *Bandit Queen*; *Saving Private Ryan*)
- the world of the space ship versus the world on Earth/planet (science fiction, e.g. *Star Wars*)
- the world of the prison versus the world outside (prison movies, e.g. *The Shawshank Redemption*)
- the world of the haunted house versus the world of home (horror, e.g. *Scream*)
- the world of safety versus the world of adventure (adventure/fantasy, e.g. *The Lord of the Rings*).

Another way of organising your characters is to assign them to different realms. For instance, you might structure your central dramatic problem around the conflicts that arise between the protagonist and key archetypes who inhabit or embody different realms. In *Basic Instinct*, the protagonist Detective Nick Curran belongs in the realm of work at the police department. His love interest, Catherine Trammel, belongs in the wild and untamed realm of her surfside beachhouse. Nick's antagonist, Beth, belongs in the same realm as Nick, the world of work. Nick's central problem is to catch a killer by moving between these realms and correctly reading the evidence he has at his disposal.

Support roles and subplots

Study the range of character types appropriate to your story and start to map your protagonist's journey according to the key figures who accompany them. Consider which realms of experience—which locations—these support characters belong to and consider how these realms will affect the mood of the story.

Usually these characters belong to various subplots. These are brief, subsidiary stories that take the protagonist on a kind of sideways journey into the parallel world of another character. Subplots will be examined in detail in Chapter 9; for now, remember that the conflict or tension between the protagonist and support roles should add more weight to the central problem, not lead us into another totally separate story world.

By assigning key support roles to different realms, you can organise the dynamics of your story to build a sense of conflict. For example, in *Thelma & Louise*, the two women drive across the dry area of the American Mid-West. Through committing a murder, they have put themselves beyond society in the no-man's land of the highway. One problem is for them to find a hiding place in this inhospitable domain.

In *The Silence of the Lambs*, we meet the young protagonist Clarice Starling in the training grounds of the FBI, where she is the only woman in her group. Her job is to track down a kidnapper in his lair, an underground basement divided into several dungeon-like areas—a metaphor for his shadowy psychology.

Clarice meets the villain, Hannibal Lecter, in a high-security prison where he is chained and restrained in a special body suit. This prison environment suggests something about the wild impulses of his character; a cannibal who requires constant restriction for the safety of those around him.

Clarice must navigate her way between these various realms. She needs to capture the kidnapper, rescue his victim, negotiate with Hannibal Lecter and carve out a role for herself as a young woman in the FBI's official environment. The barriers she must overcome in these outer realms reflect her inner struggle. Each realm of action in the outside realm reflects an element of her inner or psychological world.

A character may need or desire something but be hampered or immobilised by some inner fear or belief. The writer needs to provide concrete barriers which reveal this inner struggle and which may prevent a character from getting what they aim for.

One clever way to construct your protagonist's problem is to focus on what they *really* need, as opposed to what they desire or *think* they need. This leads the writer into the area of human psychology that governs our vanities, delusions and foibles. These character flaws make a character interesting and really human.

For instance, in *Basic Instinct*, Detective Nick Curran *aims* to solve the murder of a former rock star. His goal is to nail his chief suspect, but one barrier is his romantic feeling for her. Nick eventually *wants* to have sex with her, but this desire becomes a barrier which may prevent him from achieving his real *need* or aim: to investigate and resolve the nature of her role in a murder case.

The writer understands that what Nick *wants* is a good time with Catherine Trammel; however, what he *needs* is to solve the crime and understand her as a fellow spirit who may hold the key to the killer's identity.

In *Thelma & Louise*, Thelma aims to have a weekend away from her husband. She *wants* a break from her dull, ordinary life as a housewife. Thelma gets involved in a crime which provides a series of obstacles and barriers to her goal of a happy holiday. As it turns out, what she really *needs* is a total break from her husband and a complete change of life.

In *Breakfast at Tiffany's*, Holly *wants* to find a wealthy husband to take care of her. She falls in love with a poor writer who presents a barrier to her plan. As a result of struggling with this barrier,

71

she realises that what she really *needs* is a man who will love and nurture her for who she really is, despite her past.

Summary

We have seen how the writer can develop the protagonist's dramatic problem as a means of strengthening the screenplay on a number of levels. In summary, conflict may be structured into the drama by focusing on the various relations between:

- different ideas, goals or motives that furnish the protagonist's (and the writer's!) inner realm
- different realms or domains of the protagonist's outer environment
- the protagonist and other characters.

If the audience can identify with the protagonist and relate to the dramatic problem at hand, they are more likely to 'buy' the story as a whole. As a result of the problem and the complications it entails, the protagonist must navigate a kind of obstacle course. For instance:

- Nick Curran must endure a number of false accusations before his name is cleared (*Basic Instinct*).
- Thelma and Louise must cross the country to escape the police before their game is up (*Thelma & Louise*).
- Holly Golightly must undergo several painful reminders of her true identity, including a brush with the law before she is able to recognise one man as her true soulmate (*Breakfast at Tiffany's*).

- Clarice Starling must explore several forbidding realms before confronting the final horror that will make or break her as an FBI agent (*The Silence of the Lambs*).

Consider what problems your protagonist must face. In the next chapter, we will look at how to organise and plot these various onscreen events and conflicts using the basic building blocks of time and space.

EXERCISE 3

Character psychology

3.1   Character profiles and psychology: using your folio, try to define your protagonist's motivation—the ideas that drive them towards their goals.

It's useful to examine the conflict that may arise out of your protagonist's small vulnerabilities. These human qualities are the stuff of great comedy and drama, as they relate to universal faults that we all share. To establish a clearly defined profile for your protagonist, make notes in response to the following:

* What are the protagonist's main values, attitudes and beliefs?
* What are the protagonist's main desires, needs and goals?
* What are the protagonist's main fears, vanities, delusions and foibles?

You can explore some of these ideas in your folio by noting your answers to these key questions:

* What does the protagonist want/fear the most? How does this affect their goal?
* What or who is the source of the problem or dilemma that the protagonist must confront?
* What is the protagonist's internal problem?
* What is the protagonist's external problem?
* What is the protagonist's central problem or dilemma?

3.2   The protagonist's inner and outer realms: What is the protagonist's present world? Locate them in an interesting environment or profession that reflects some aspect of their motivation and psychological make-up. Make notes on how this outer world may help you to articulate aspects of their inner world or psychology.

3.3   Support characterisation: Even before they are sure of their story, good writers will draft extensive character biographies for all key characters as a way of preparing for their first screenplay draft. In fact, many ideas for plot and story come out of this initial research phase, where the characters start to take on a life of their own.

While writing character biographies, study the range of character types that are appropriate to your story. You may begin to map your protagonist's journey according to the key figures who accompany them. These key roles may include generic or archetypal figures such as:

* buddy
* mentor
* parent
* child
* love interest
* villain

Write a one-page sketch on the key characters—family, lovers, antagonists—who may become your key support roles.

* Can you articulate the concepts, themes or ideas that they represent to an audience?
* What do they tell us about the protagonist and their problem? For example, a jockey at the racetrack enters the winner's circle and is threatened by an angry rival—this is a story about gambling; about the passions of sport; about the competitive spirit of people trained to win at all costs.

4

Time is the basic building block

Chapter objective

To differentiate between two crucial dimensions: the 'time of the tale' and the 'time of the telling'.

In the previous chapter, we examined how the writer can create character biography, or backstory, out of events and actions that happen 'in the past' of that character's offscreen world. This backstory may then be used by the writer to inform action in the 'present' world—the world the audience sees onscreen.

We also examined character psychology and motivation to see how human flaws, self-delusion and weakness can produce conflict and dramatic problems. Conflict can arise when needs and desire are confused. It can also arise when fear or foibles prevent the protagonist from achieving their goals.

We have seen how a clash between the protagonist's realms of action may contribute to their central dramatic problem. We have examined how this problem may drive the plot and give it shape.

Writing for film is really about creating logical sequences of events and action. In this chapter, we will examine both classic and alternative techniques in plotting that allow you to achieve this.

A screenwriter must develop the skill and experience required to manipulate story chronology. As with the mastery of any craft or art form, the first step is to understand fully how such conventions work. Only then is it possible to play with or subvert the accepted form and produce a more challenging screenplay.

In this chapter, we will describe the plot as a schedule of events that occur over three acts which represent the beginning, middle and end of the narrative or story. We also focus on one of your main jobs as writer: to organise these events over two dimensions—space and time. So let's identify some of the ways you can manipulate space and time in a screenplay.

Magical and musical elements

The creation of both music and film requires attention to the careful ordering of moments in time. Western music is structured around the number of beats per bar. In a similar way, time is the basic building block of cinema. The screenwriter, like the composer, helps an audience to pass time using a highly structured language. In order to substitute one set of events (reality) for another (story 'reality'), the screenwriter, like the composer, must play tricks with the audience's perception of time.

This process involves more than 'passing the time' for the audience; it involves creating various illusions. The screenwriter's basic tools include elements of sight and sound which are manipulated in quite magical ways. The word 'magic' is appropriate here, as the filmed image and the filmed story both rely on various kinds of technical illusion to achieve their overall effect.

The writer must rely on several tricks of the trade to create the illusion of 'reality' onscreen. Some of the most crucial ingredients in your toolbox concern the management of time. The process of writing for film requires the writer to subvert the passage of time in the 'real' world.

When organising the schedule of events and action in their story, the screenwriter's job is to carefully time or pace the telling of the story—to select events and sequence them over three acts according to the audience's viewpoint. As we have already discussed, much of this process occurs beyond the conscious awareness of the audience. When happily cocooned inside the cinema or at home with their video player, the audience forgets they are watching a theatrical concoction. They will suspend their disbelief and treat the film's illusions as a kind of 'reality'.

Chronology of the plot

As we have seen, your protagonist may have a long and complicated backstory leading backwards into their childhood or early life. The writer must consider which parts of the protagonist's backstory they wish to reveal in the limited time available onscreen. This means the writer must select and plan the order of events.

The writer must also plot out the complex interconnections between characters and situations onscreen. Central to all this, the writer must plan the amount of screen time they will take to reveal different aspects of the plot.

Let's examine some basic plotting techniques that help the writer to organise the plot chronology.

. The chronology of the plot refers to the way the passage of time is structured around two distinct but interrelated time frames sometimes known as the *time of the tale* and the *time of the telling*. The writer must balance these time frames and pace the action within a three-act structure that covers the beginning, middle and end of the overall story.

1 *The time of the tale describes a timeline for the protagonist's onscreen journey.* It is the time frame made up of events, episodes and moments from the protagonist's experience. These moments must be ordered as scenes by the writer, who selects them from the protagonist's entire 'offscreen' backstory or biography. The writer must decide whether the time of the tale will represent days, weeks or years of the protagonist's journey.

2 *The time of the telling describes a timeline for the audience as they sit watching in the cinema or at home.* This time frame describes the way the screen time is divided to accommodate the various moments and scenes from the time of the tale. The writer must decide how to unfold the story events according to acts or turning points that help to organise the highs and lows of the character's arc or journey. The writer must structure this time frame according to the available screen time.

It is the writer's job to check the pace of the plot so that the time of the tale balances with the time of the telling. Together, these two time frames are held in balance by the writer to make up the chronology of the story.

It is one of the writer's most difficult jobs to arrange the onscreen events so that the story unfolds dramatically within a clearly defined time frame. Whether they are writing a full-length feature script or a five-minute short, the writer must carefully manipulate the audience's perception of time. They may create various illusions along the way, manipulating onscreen time so that the audience has an almost timeless or dreamlike experience.

Ideally, the audience should not be too aware of the cinematic illusions they are observing while sitting in the cinema. Such illusions are treated in different ways within different genres or types of film story. In some types of story, the plot appears to flow as if events were unfolding in 'real' time as part of a timeless, dreamlike state. In other genres, the audience may be 'on the edge of their seats', anxious with suspense, and actively piecing together the clues and the outcomes of the story.

We have borrowed many of our illusions of time from realist theatre and literature of the classic epoch. Of course, other approaches are possible, but the writer must take care not to upset audience expectations without fully understanding the nature of the mechanism they are dealing with.

The main challenge for the writer is to fabricate a strong system of reasons to support the action and the conflict. Events must be set up so that their underlying causes are visible to the audience. The relations between characters, locations and situations must be governed by a system of cause and effect. This system ensures that the plot will be logical and believable.

To create a logical story, the writer must contain and organise all the cause-and-effect relations between onscreen characters, locations and events. You will need to create a kind of schedule of events and scenes that unfolds naturally so that the audience reads the story as 'real', or at least credible.

Above all, you need to be familiar with the requirements of the genre you are working in. For instance, the rules relating to the chronology of a suspense story will be highly specific and technical, while those relating to a drama or comedy will be more transparent and easy to manage. The writer needs to be aware of how each specific genre will allow for different constraints and opportunities in the treatment of time.

In summary, the writer must achieve a balance between the time of the tale and the time of the telling. You may consider how to manage the time of the tale—which parts of the protagonist's story you wish to reveal and in which order. You must also plan the amount of time you will take to do so.

From the audience viewpoint, it is essential that the plot makes sense. The last thing you want is for an audience to walk out of the cinema scratching their heads and wondering, 'What was all *that* about?'

Plot logic

All the cause-and-effect relations between onscreen characters, locations and events must be organised within a kind of schedule. The writer must figure out how the sequences of scenes can be developed to explain the onscreen events.

Think of your screenplay on a page-by-page or minute-by-minute basis. One easy rule of thumb is to remember that, on average, to enact one page of the screenplay document takes up to one minute of screen-time. This means that if you are writing page 25 of your properly formatted script, your story is approximately 25 minutes into the action.

Traditional Western dramas and comedies usually describe the journey of the protagonist as it unfolds from the past into the present and future in a simple, linear sequence.

Let's look closely at the need to keep your story moving forward. The audience is focused on what happens *next* in the story. Depending on the genre, they may also be interested in figuring out what happened *before*, in the past. For instance, in the thriller and mystery/suspense genres, the unseen, offscreen areas of the backstory or the past are often the subject of intense scrutiny by the protagonist (the detective) and the audience.

However, it is important to note that in most other genres, audience suspense is focused not on the past but on the present and future action. This means that the writer needs to keep the audience tuned-in, to keep them guessing as to what will happen next. If too many of the key events of the plot happen offscreen in the protagonist's backstory, the audience can lose interest or lose track of the plot.

The audience needs to feel in touch with current events onscreen in front of them. Thus, the best way to keep an audience interested is to give them story clues and action. As with television, the favoured illusion is that the action occurs as if 'live', onscreen, happening right now. For this reason, the writer's main task is to keep the action moving forward in the present scenario.

Organising your chronology

According to the story outline you have developed, your protagonist's journey may take place over days, weeks, months or years. But your job is to ensure that this entire story is condensed, compressed, abbreviated and compacted into around 100 minutes of screen-time. It is your job to select key events and situations from within a huge continuum that is the protagonist's 'life' and code them into a mere 100 or so pages of script.

How are we to achieve this difficult ratio of action into minutes? The classic approach of mainstream screenwriting is to manipulate the story chronology so that the protagonist's 'reality' unfolds before the audience in an almost dreamlike way where time is no object. The screenwriter generally follows the same linear order of 'real life'. First something happens in the life of the protagonist; then, an hour, a day or a year later, something else happens to build the story in a linear way.

Obviously the writer can only reveal the tip of the iceberg— only two minutes of the protagonist's busy wedding day may be shown, while the rest of that day is left out. We can cut from a scene of the wedding ceremony to a scene of the honeymoon, some days later. Or we can cut from the wedding, straight to the divorce court, years later down the storytelling track. This means that, from the audience's viewpoint, the protagonist may appear to undergo weeks, or even years, worth of experience in a matter of minutes.

The audience can bridge such large chronological gaps in their imagination. Due to our familiarity with strong linear narrative traditions, we are used to a scheme where once-upon-a-time something happens, then another thing—followed by many ups and downs. Finally, there is an ending to the story. The audience instinctively understands (without having to analyse how or why) that, in classic linear mode, some events will be dropped and others will be emphasised, depending on the needs of the storyteller to make a point.

The demanding economy of screen-time, which means that one minute equals one page of the screenplay, puts the writer under incredible pressure to express enormous ideas and copious information within an extremely brief window or opening. Unlike the novelist, who has pages and pages in which to express ideas, action and emotion, the screenwriter is limited to a much more disciplined framework. Every word must be carefully selected in order to maximise its effect within the whole. Every word—like a musical note—must also be selected in relation to the overall timing of the plot.

The unity of space and time

To achieve dramatic effects within the constraints of onscreen and offscreen time, the writer must treat time, next to character psychology, as the basic material of the plot.

If we are talking about drama or comedy, it pays the writer *not* to spread the chronology of a story over too many episodes, years and locations. A broad epic sweep may work for some particular genres (such as historical biography or epic); in general, however, drawing the story out over a long period in the protagonist's life tends to diffuse the sense of urgency and suspense. It's not a good idea to spread the action over 30 locations and three decades in a character's life. Not only would such a story cost a fortune to produce, but the writer also risks spreading the dramatic content over too large a canvas.

For most dramatic purposes, it works best for the writer to limit the time of the protagonist's tale. This helps to maintain the intensity of the story as well as audience interest in the outcomes of the story.

Ancient storytellers and dramatists such as Aristotle understood centuries ago that it is most effective for the writer to look at a single episode or era in the protagonist's life. This ensures that the time of the protagonist's tale is short (not decades in a lifetime) and the setting is limited to a manageable scope.

Usually, the writer must focus on the development of a single, central dramatic problem and play the drama out in human terms that we are all familiar with—how does our protagonist feel *now*, and what will happen *next*?

We have seen that it is more dramatic for a problem to occur in the 'here and now' of screen-time, rather than to leave it in the distant past of the backstory, which may remain invisible to the audience. For that reason, it may be most effective to condense your action down to three key days or weeks in the life of the subject and to pack these days with action and suspense.

Poetic licence can be used to bring together events which, in your backstory, may have occurred years apart. By bringing these incidents and events closer together in time, you create a sense of immediacy. For instance, the writer may condense the time frame of the plot so that things which in the backstory occurred years ago, actually occur just 'yesterday' in the protagonist's onscreen world.

In this way, the writer learns to select from a large body of events and ideas, re-editing them in time so that the most interesting events happen onscreen where the audience can see them. Observing this general rule helps to promote a sense of urgency, of powerful, 'high-impact' drama and of continuity between episodes in the plot.

This basic dramatic theory is known as 'maintaining the unity of time and space in the drama'. The technique stretches back to theatre in the time of Aristotle. In those days, the protagonist's drama was usually depicted within the time frame of a single day's action. It is still a general rule of suspense that drama is most effective when focused around a single episode or era in the protagonist's life—a single key event (or cluster of events) that acts as a prism or focus for the protagonist in action.

Aristotle explains in *Poetics* that a beautiful story is like 'a beautiful object . . . it must not only have an orderly arrangement of parts, but must also be of a certain magnitude; for beauty depends on magnitude and order'.

So Aristotle suggests that the writer must observe the proper proportion of a story and its parts: 'A certain magnitude is necessary . . . which may be easily embraced in one view; so in the plot, a certain length is necessary . . . which can be easily embraced by the memory.'

One key to this is that the events depicted on stage in the classic comedy or drama will be depicted within what Aristotle calls 'the unity of space and time'. By this he means that the writer must portray 'the sequence of events according to the law of probability or necessity'. In other words, the sequence must make sense according to the laws that govern our ordinary lives. At the same time, it needs to depict a dramatic and marked change in the life of the protagonist: 'The sequence will admit of a change from bad fortune to good, or from good fortune to bad.'

Aristotle has further tips for the dramatist that are relevant to the screenwriter. He recognises that a protagonist's backstory may contain 'infinitely various' incidents and actions. However, the writer doesn't need to include *all* the adventures of their hero or heroine. Aristotle points out that the great poet Homer, when writing the adventures of Odysseus, didn't include *all* the adventures of his hero. He only included those incidents between which there was a necessary and probable connection.

'Homer made *The Odyssey* centre around an action that in our sense of the word is one.' Aristotle knew that drama, like sculpture and painting, was the imitation of a single action, 'a whole, structural union of the parts'. He also points out the importance of integrating these parts so that nothing is superfluous or without function in the structure of the story. This means that the writer must test each strand of the story to ensure that 'if any one of these parts is displaced or removed, the whole will be disjointed and disturbed. For a thing whose presence or absence makes no visible difference, is not an organic part of the whole.' This simple but effective rule suggests that if there are story elements that are not crucial to your plot, they can be cut.

Aristotle's wisdom about portraying drama within a narrow, manageable time frame is still observed as the key to dramatic suspense in mainstream cinema. For instance, the thriller, drama, action and suspense genres tend to work within a highly coherent, linear chronological style where the writer observes Aristotle's unity of space and time.

Exposition and backstory

With first-time writers, there is often a temptation to expand 'the time of the tale'. For instance, when writing about your protagonist in your folio, you may be intrigued by childhood events in the protagonist's journey. You may then want to structure your story using flashbacks to include episodes that occurred in the distant past. Rather than depicting events in the past, you may try to keep some unity in your story by devoting attention to character psychology in the present context. The tools to achieve this are known as exposition and backstory.

Character backstory is extremely relevant to every aspect of a screenplay, especially to the chronology. The writer must add depth and weight and authenticity to characters and situations by providing glimpses of their past using visual or verbal clues.

This means that, rather than spreading the focus of your story too wide, you can use exposition to tell the audience how the protagonist's early life now affects their life in the here and now.

This is known as providing exposition; it is a way of exposing the character's backstory by revealing elements of their history in creative ways onscreen.

You can add much depth to your character by providing information about their past. We will discuss the use of flashbacks in some detail in the next chapter. For now, it's worth considering the flashback a rather awkward device for developing both character and plot. Rather than flashing back, the writer can translate some of the crucial backstory material into the 'now' using various forms of exposition. To achieve this, the writer needs to consider time as a fluid resource that can be shifted and shaped according to the needs of the story.

Let's discuss how you can structure quite detailed information about the past into images, action and dialogue.

In *Basic Instinct*, crucial backstory about the murder suspect Catherine Trammel is delivered verbally, as well as by scenes featuring information about the character's past life. Some scenes depict clippings from magazine articles that feature pictures of the character, set in the past. Other vital backstory is structured into police records which are revealed via computer files onscreen and discussed as a matter of police procedure by the protagonist and his colleagues. In this way, the audience learns crucial details about the chief suspect. We learn the clues that will help to structure the onscreen journey of the protagonist, Detective Nick Curran.

The mystery and thriller genres allow for a special protagonist (often the detective) to closely examine and reveal the backstory of one or more other characters. However, for the purposes of most drama and comedy, the action generally needs to emphasise the present context, keeping the unity of space and time to a narrow time frame.

In *Thelma & Louise*, the time of the tale is very limited, as the women go on holiday, commit several crimes, make their escape and get caught, all within the space of a two-week period. The writer correctly assumes that if the action is spread out over months or years, we will lose our sense of the protagonists' main problem: their urgent need to escape.

In contrast, the epic, biography and science fiction genres allow a writer to range over a much wider span of time. We may follow the course of a family dynasty over generations, or follow the journey of a single character from youth to adulthood. Within this epic genre, it is acceptable to range over a wide time frame that may depict a character's lifetime with a large historical canvas as background.

In this way, the writer may explain how dynasties evolve, how wars are won and lost, how love can be won and lost over the course of a lifetime, how history repeats itself, and so on. Such long treks through time are often appropriate to the TV mini-series genre or the epic movie, where there is more screen-time available for the writer to create an extended chronology.

You have probably written a long and fascinating backstory for your main character. One challenge is to rearrange the chronology of what you have written so that the key dramatic incidents from the protagonist's (offscreen) past can find their way into the present action (onscreen). If the main action of your plot takes place in the protagonist's adulthood, it's not a good idea to open with the protagonist as a child or to include a flashback to earlier days. However, there is no reason why you cannot recontextualise moments of your protagonist's past by simply shifting them into the present.

Not everything that you first envisage as backstory belongs in the past. Become an astute editor of your own work. Consider shifting interesting moments around freely within your screenplay so that time becomes more fluid.

To create an interesting story within the constraints of time, the writer must often condense or compress the action. At different points in the story, they may also decide to extend or lengthen time, or to skip over time or slow it down in order to draw the audience's attention to a significant moment.

The writer can be quite bold in shifting gears with chronology. Consider the past, present and future as a plastic, malleable entity, rather than as a rigid, linear structure. For example, let's say that you have finished the backstory for your latest character, a pyromaniac who likes to steal fire-trucks. The backstory may suggest that your protagonist was traumatised at age fifteen when he was caught lighting a fire by a fireman. Why not move that incident into the present? It is more interesting for an audience to see such a dramatic and colourful moment acted out by an adult today, rather than just mentioned in dialogue as a piece of backstory or exposition.

Your backstory often contains gems of action that can be hauled forward into the present as part of the onscreen action. A flexible approach to chronology will allow you to envisage how such shifts may be creatively organised within the narrow requirements of the classic three-act structure.

One principle worth remembering is that key moments in the distant past of a character's early life could be used profitably in the present to help move the action along. The trick is to recognise which material you have imagined in the past realm needs to be brought forward into the present realm to structure the onscreen action.

In older-style films, the flashback was often employed to give a glimpse of a character's past. These days, however, writers tend to bring the past into the present using a variety of techniques that refer us to character backstory.

In the film *Rain Man*, there is a striking example of how the writers Ronald Bass and Barry Morrow have used character backstory to enrich the drama. The writer avoids any clunky flashbacks by structuring past action into the present in a very dramatic way.

In the final act, the two Babbitt brothers, played by Tom Cruise and Dustin Hoffman, are in a bathroom where one is filling the tub with water. As his brother turns on the tap, the noise seems to send the Hoffman character into a kind of fit. As the scene develops, it becomes apparent that he is reliving the traumatic memory of a bathtime event in his childhood. In this dramatic moment, the Hoffman character relives the past onscreen, effectively bringing an event that happened 30 years previously, into the immediate present. As Hoffman relives his early trauma, his brother looks on, slowly putting together the pieces of his story in the same way that the audience does. Both brothers, in this moment, recall the key event that has structured their relationship. They both recall a childhood scene in which one brother first called the other 'Rain man'.

Rather than literally taking us back to that moment in the past, the writers powerfully evoke this crucial piece of backstory by using action in the present. The scene provides the missing link in solving the mystery of the brothers' entire relationship and that of the film's title.

If the writers had presented this key scene in flashback form, they would have had to depart from the present flow of action, signal the use of a flashback device and use a different pair of (child) actors. This would immediately signal to the audience that they are entering a different time zone, as well as a different stylistic zone. Rather than disturb the unity and integrity of space and time in this way, the writers have managed to maintain the forward flow of the story. Thus, they can bring the past into the present very effectively and with great emotional impact.

New writers are often tempted to use flashbacks to make direct use of the rich backstory they have created during their research. However, if you are tempted to use flashbacks, ask yourself how you can achieve similar dramatic results by bringing action from the past into the present in a convincing way. The audience isn't so interested in what happened yesterday. They are even less interested in what happened years ago. They are more interested in what will happen *next* than in what transpired yesterday.

Historical epics

Big leaps in time may be necessary when describing the historical sweep of large or important figures in history. Flashes forward and back may be used as a means of traversing decades and continents. They are appropriate to describe the larger movements of an epoch or a dynasty or a famous individual who reflects or is pivotal to historical change.

When working on an historical biography or epic story, the audience experiences the past in the 'now'. In this special genre, it is permissible for the writer to carve wide patterns in the story chronology.

Take, for instance, the film biography (known also as a 'biopic') of *Gandhi*. In this film, the action covers five decades in the life of the great Indian activist and politician.

The first act of *Gandhi* opens with a crowded street scene in which the central character, Gandhi, appears as an old man in India. He is shot dead by a mysterious assassin. We immediately flash back to the protagonist as a young man, visiting South Africa. The action then works through the next five decades and ends finally with a repetition of the assassination scene we saw in the first five minutes.

In *Gandhi*, the epic span of the protagonist's life story is framed by an identical prologue and epilogue that detail his tragic death. In this very neat structural framework, the story ends where it began, having explained along the way many of the reasons for the tragic ending.

The writer reveals Gandhi's death early in the introductory passage as a kind of flash-forward to the story's logical ending. All of this occurs in the first frames of the film. We then return to 'the present', the logical beginning of the story, which occurs way back in the past. We flash back to Gandhi's youth and his early career in South Africa before moving forward in a straight, linear order over five decades and several key incidents in his life and career. The writer closes the story on the same assassination scene. Only now, this scene appears to be in 'logical' chronological order.

In this way the writer uses the flash-forward creatively, inviting us to inspect the story action for clues as to the reasons for the tragedy. The writer provides us with the reasons behind the assassination that stretch back into the distant past. This complex story structure invites us to conclude that the tragedy was somehow inevitable.

We have seen that flashes forward and back may be useful in allowing the writer to make an epic narrative sweep across decades and continents. Flashbacks and flash-forwards are also useful in mystery/suspense, where the audience may need complex exposition or contextual information in order to gather the clues that create suspense and intrigue. For most drama and comedy genres, however, the flashback and flash-forward remain somewhat clumsy methods of bringing backstory to the viewer. The next chapter will discuss this further and offer hints on how good writers can structure incidents from the past into the present dramatic framework. This is achieved by focusing always on the current action as it plays out onscreen.

Remember that whatever the epoch or era in which your story is set, your audience will want to see action *in the present*; they need to know what happens *now* and what happens *next*.

EXERCISE 4

Plot chronology

4.1 Look at your folio and consider the key moments in the distant past of your protagonist's early life. Remember that most of this information and research won't make it on to the screen as part of the action.

To begin organising the time frame of your story, you must be very focused in creating and selecting the moments you will depict onscreen. These moments may be structured into scenes as part of dialogue or exposition. The rest of your backstory material can be useful as your personal research material—an important resource to help you generate the plot and understand the characters. Your backstory may also assist you to make decisions about what your characters would or wouldn't do in certain situations.

a. Recall your premise: What story values are of importance to the protagonist's journey?

b. Which period of the subject's life will you depict?

c. Which episodes and details will you include from your backstory?

d. Consider the order or sequence in which all this will appear onscreen.

e. Consider how much screen-time you might devote to each episode or scene.

*Remember also that you are limited by the standard economy: one page of screenplay format equals roughly one minute of screentime.

4.2 Now select three key moments or scenes in the life of the protagonist whom you have chosen as the focus for the story. Each of these will represent a key moment in either the beginning, middle or end of your story. They will help you to outline 'the time of the tale'.

* Remember that some of the material you have imagined in the past realm may be easily brought forward into the present realm to structure the onscreen action.

95

5

Devices for manipulating story chronology

Chapter objective

To identify many of the time/space elements that allow the writer to manipulate time both onscreen and offscreen.

The previous chapters outlined the rules of classic chronology. Audiences are used to the linear mode and can lose their sense of the action quite easily if the writer uses too many radical tricks of the trade. This means that your story chronology must make sense. Each scene must follow logically from the ones that precede it. Each scene must also foreshadow or build up to the scenes that follow.

In this chapter we discuss alternative methods for the treatment of space and time. In these models, the straightforward development of the protagonist's singular arc is challenged by a more fragmented, parallel, or at times circular, approach to plot and chronology. Films discussed include *The Matrix*, *Sliding Doors*, *Gandhi*, *Pulp Fiction* and *Run Lola Run*.

Many such late-20th century films manipulate the time frames or chronology of stories to create a kind of synchronicity between characters and events. This technique allows the audience to pause and examine how different characters cope with the same situations at different points along the time/space continuum.

This kind of complexity reflects the multi-layered reality (or realities) that people now inhabit, especially in urban societies. It suggests that our view of ourselves may be evolving to include the possibility of more than one, strictly linear, view of how space and time operate. Some may say that cinema has at last caught up with the insights of Einstein, for whom space and time are absolutely relative. Others may see this splintering of Aristotle's classic unities as a radical treatment of screen-time and space which seems to suggest that we each inhabit a series of parallel universes, where time and location are fluid.

Physics aside, the popular success of such screenplays suggests that it is up to the writer to be creative. In many ways, from the writer's viewpoint, this sequencing process is rather like writing music. The basic process is about managing the passage of time. It is about the writer selecting moments and orchestrating them, creating moments of calm and excitement, then building these up towards climaxes both for the actors on the sound stage and for the audience in the cinema. This manipulation of time creates emotion, memory and suspense—the basic units of the cinematic experience.

Let's focus now on the various devices available to the writer which can help you to manipulate the pacing, chronology and sequencing of your scenes. These technical forms will be discussed in detail and include:

- locations and setting
- montage
- flashbacks and flash-forwards
- deadlines, ticking clocks and high-stakes dilemmas

- parallel action
- circular or non-linear chronology.

Locations and setting

Careful attention to your locations and setting can convey a lot of information about chronology and the passage of time. Time can be slowed down or stopped with the freeze frame or the long take, where each second seems to be packed with significance for the audience. The simple fade is often used to suggest the passage of time and its effect on characters and the story. For instance, we might fade out of a scene by focusing on the image of an apple tree in flower. The next scene may fade up on the same tree, now bare and frozen in winter. The audience will now assume that several months—whole seasons—have passed between these two scenes.

We may end one scene with our protagonist dressed in rags and with long hair and a beard. In order to convey information about the passage of time or a radical change, the next scene may show the same protagonist now cleanly shaven, with a neat haircut and wearing a suit. The visual changes alone will invite the audience to ask questions and draw conclusions about what has happened in the meantime. Remember that film is a visual medium. It is vital to *show* psychological change or *illustrate* the passage of time, rather than just *talk* about it.

Montage

Montage is a French term that refers to the process of assembling something from several elements—that is, making a whole out of parts or fragments. Montage describes the way much complex information can be conveyed to the audience in a kind of visual shorthand. It may describe a sequence of images which show the rapid passage of time, or the completion of several complex actions with a brief glimpse at each.

The master film-maker Sergei Eisenstein wrote in 1938 that montage was defined as the juxtaposition of contrasts. He points out the astonishing properties and effects of montage as 'two film pieces of any kind, placed together, inevitably combine into a new concept, a new quality, arising out of their juxtaposition'. According to Eisenstein, clever montage allows the film-maker or storyteller to create inferences, riddles, contradictions and surprises for the audience. He notes that if the writer puts the image of a woman weeping next to the image of a grave, the inference is that she is the widow mourning for her husband. However, the film-maker may surprise us in the next scene by revealing that in fact it was her lover she was grieving for. (Einsenstein 1970, p. 14).

The montage may also be used to summarise a long or complex chain of events, places and people. In this way, it provides a kind of summary or list of brief visual vignettes or snapshots. The montage can help a writer take the audience through an extended period in the time of the tale. This compilation of images can convey quite complex information about the plot in a short space of time and in just a few pages in your script.

A brilliant example of montage is in Frank Capra's film, *Mr Smith Goes to Washington* (1939). The young and unsophisticated Jefferson Smith (Jimmy Stewart) arrives in Washington from a small country town. He is so excited about seeing his country's capital city that he leaves his companions behind to go on a sightseeing bus tour. This tour is covered in a beautiful visual montage of shots created especially for the film by the émigré Russian film-maker, Slavko Vorkapich.

The images and the accompanying music-mix present a powerful celebration of the United States' democratic heroes (including George Washington, Thomas Jefferson and Abraham Lincoln). The montage accomplishes a number of things. It summarises a piece of the storyline, and provides character depth and motivation to Stewart's Jefferson Smith character. The selection and sequence of images in this montage also presents a crucial theme that the film is concerned with: the ideal of democracy in North American history.

Another example of montage is found in *The Matrix*, a science fiction adventure that depicts a futuristic world as if through the looking glass. The scene below comes from an early draft of the script. In the scene, Morpheus, the leader of the revolutionary cyber-team, explains to Neo, the unwilling hero, that the world as we know it is purely illusion. The visual montage is played out as a fast-moving series of extraordinary images that take us to various locations in space and time as Morpheus's voice rolls on:

                              NEO
          This isn't real?

                           MORPHEUS
          What is real? How do you define real? If you're
          talking about your senses, what you feel, taste,
          smell, or see, then all you're talking about are elec-
          trical signals interpreted by your brain.

     He picks up a remote control and clicks on the television.
     We drift through the Windy City circa 1996.

MORPHEUS

This is the Chicago you know. Chicago as it was at the end of the twentieth century. This Chicago exists only as part of a neural-interactive simulation that we call the Matrix.

We glide at the television as he changes the channel.

MORPHEUS

You have been living inside Baulliaurd's vision, inside the map, not the territory. This is Chicago as it exists today.

The sky is an endless sea of black and green bile. The earth, scorched and split like burnt flesh, spreads out beneath us as we enter the television.

MORPHEUS

'The desert of the real.'

In the distance, we see the ruins of a future Chicago protruding from the wasteland like the blackened ribs of a long-dead corpse.

MORPHEUS

We are, right now, miles below the earth's surface. The only place humans can survive outside the Matrix is underground.

Still moving, we turn and find Neo and Morpheus; the chair's now sitting in the middle of the black desert. Dizzy, Neo holds onto the chair.

NEO

What happened?

MORPHEUS

It started early in the twenty-first century, with the
birth of artificial intelligence, a singular conscious-
ness that spawned an entire race of machines.

In his sunglasses, we see storm clouds gather.

MORPHEUS

At first all they wanted was to be treated as equals,
entitled to the same human inalienable rights.
Whatever they were given, it was not enough.

In the circular window of the glasses, explosions light up a
bloody battle field.

MORPHEUS

We don't know who struck first. Us or them. But
sometime at the end of the twenty-first century the
battle was joined.

We move into his glasses and the war surrounds us.

MORPHEUS

The war raged for generations and turned the face
of our planet from green and blue to black and red.

At last we see the Sentinels; killing machines that are at once
terrifying and beautiful. They have an organic architecture like
a microbiotic organism, that is perpetually in motion.

The Sentinel cracks the body armor of a soldier, splitting open
the soft, stearing meat inside.

MORPHEUS

It scorched and burned the sky. Without the sun, the machines sought out a new energy source to survive.

The Sentinel locks up, as heat lightning of black ink bursts against the sky, spreading into a permanent cloud of stain.

MORPHEUS

They discovered a new form of fusion. All that was required to initiate the reaction was a small electric charge. Throughout human history we have been dependent on machines to survive. Fate, it seems, is not without a sense of irony.

We return to the power plant that Neo escaped from where we see human beings looking almost blissful in their gelatin cocoons.

MORPHEUS

The human body generates more bio-electricity than a 120-volt battery and over 25,000 B.T.U.'s of body heat.

Outside, spreading all around the power plant, beneath a breathing greenhouse, are the growing fields.

MORPHEUS

We are, as an energy source, easily renewable and completely recyclable, the dead liquified and fed intravenously to the living.

Huge farm-like reapers are harvesting the crop.

> MORPHEUS
>
> All they needed to control this new battery was something to occupy our mind.

We see inside a clear tubular husk. Floating in viscous fluid, there is a human fetus; its soft skull already growing around the brain-jack.

> MORPHEUS
>
> And so they built a prison out of our past, wired it to our brains and turned us into slaves.

We pull back to find the image is now on the television and we are again inside the white space of the Construct.

> NEO
>
> No! I don't believe it! It's not possible!

© 2000 by Warner Bros. Inc

We see here how a successful montage is achieved through a process of selection, elimination, combination and assemblage of images. In this example, the images aren't placed in any recognisable chronological sequence, but are processed as if through the prism of a TV screen, suggesting the crucial role of the mass media in shaping the story world. But there is more at play here, as we see the reflection of this screen in Morpheus's sunglasses. In this way, the montage conveys information about point-of-view, suggesting that we see the world onscreen through the eyes of the characters according to their different vantage points. At the same time, the montage and the special effects reinforce a key theme. They suggest that we can never quite believe the evidence of our eyes when the play of image, reflection and surfaces seems to create one illusion after another.

The process of assembling wholes and eliminating pieces is crucial to the depth and breadth of a finished film. Montage allows the writer to compress time, while allowing the audience to glimpse large vistas of both space and time. Montage provides snapshots of 'the big picture'. In this example from *The Matrix*, the visual montage describes centuries of history in two minutes of screen-time.

There is much poetry involved in the selection and juxtaposition of such visual details which convey a wealth of meaning using a few images that are highly expressive.

Flashbacks and flash-forwards

We have seen how the flashback and the flash-forward allow the writer to shift the action backward or forward in time. They can provide the audience with information about backstory or preview a future context. Such devices are usually governed by the rules of the genre the writer is working in and are more acceptable in some genres (fantasy, science fiction) than in others.

From the 1930s to the 1960s, the favoured Hollywood techniques for indicating a shift to the past included the use of harp music, a wavering screen, flashing calendar pages, and the use of black and white footage. In the 1970s and 1980s, it became more common to use graphic subtitles to signpost a transition, such as 'Ten years later' or 'The next year'.

General industry standards suggest that it may not be a good idea to intrude on the screen-space using clunky devices such as these. They can disturb the flow of the story and are a rather awkward way of skipping forward or back in your chronology. All of this reminds the audience that they are watching a set-up and disturbs the smooth, dreamlike unfolding of the narrative. As a general rule, it is more interesting for the audience to observe the protagonist's problem being played out in the here and now, than to be worrying about something they cannot see that happened years ago.

Of course, this rule of thumb depends on which genre you are working in. If you are developing a mystery script, where clues often depend on the audience's understanding of the backstory, the use of flashbacks may be appropriate.

Mystery and suspense genres rely on a kind of game between the writer and the audience. The writer sets up a number of clues and then pays them off within a well-organised framework. This is perhaps the most technically challenging genre to write and requires the use of special formulas. Chronology is central to all this. The writer must balance the timing of the clues and must pay off various subplots in order to drive the story forward and create audience suspense so that they ask, 'What will happen next?'

Fantasy and science fiction films often feature time-travel as a staple story element. Important films such as *Solaris*, *2001: A Space Odyssey*, *Titanic* and *Terminator* challenge our perception of time and space by making large leaps forward and back in chronology. Such devices are also useful where they may help the writer to establish a sense of 'history' for their special story world.

In fantasy and science fiction, quite radical shifts in time and space may be central to the storyline. The comedy genre also manipulates our sense of time to good effect. Many gags are created by playing with chronology. Popular hits such as *Austin Powers* and *Back to the Future* deliberately play with our sense of time, using time-travel as an important story element. These contemporary scripts often use flash-forwards and flashbacks to create a new 'crossover genre' that bridges comedy and science fiction. At the same time, they are based on one of science fiction's oldest and most traditional motifs, the time machine.

In the popular science fiction hit, *The Matrix*, the protagonist named Neo moves between different time zones and different 'realities'. These shifts are signalled by changes in location and costume, and by the very consistent use of special effects that signal a shift between Neo's 'real' world and the computer-generated worlds of 'the Matrix' system. Here the protagonist isn't flashing back and forth in a linear mode, but is transported across different realities that exist in parallel universes.

In the comedy *Parenthood*, the writer uses a powerful opening device that includes a big flash-forward. The story opens at a baseball park, with the protagonist arriving as a child with his father. Soon after, we flash forward to the same baseball park years later. The boy is now an adult and is leaving the game with his own children in tow.

In this case, the writer uses the flash-forward device to signal more than a change in character and setting. It may signal something to us about the overall premise of the story—ideas about the continuity of tradition from generation to generation, and so on.

The shift from boy to man is not a realistic one in the opening of *Parenthood*. The boy in question delivers some very surreal and grown-up dialogue before disappearing to be replaced with his adult 'self'. However, a comedy audience will happily 'suspend their disbelief' in such a context. That is, they will forgive the writer for stretching the limits of credibility for the sake of a laugh or a special effect. The drama audience, however, may not be so forgiving.

Dramatic writers can manipulate space or time to achieve some tricky effects but need to be aware that any major departures from 'straight' logical chronology can test the audience's credulity and patience. No matter what the genre, it is never a good idea to confuse your audience. Remain aware that to create good suspense and mystery, the writer needs to be extremely clear in the ordering of story chronology. It is fine to pose thorny logical problems for the audience to solve; that is the essence of good mystery technique. However, the writer should organise the twists and turns of the story with great care. Mystery and confusion are not the same thing.

In general, the logical context of the plot, the subplots and the chronology needs to be well planned and watertight so that the audience has a clear view of the story components and how they work.

It is considered risky for the writer to mess around with linear chronology, for this is to meddle with the basic building blocks of our linear storytelling traditions. In classic narrative, the linear framework means that events need to be presented in a logical manner so that the audience can put together the story with confidence. The chronology of films such as *The Matrix* and *Back to the Future* are organised very carefully within the rules of the science fiction genre, which provide an opportunity to 'play' with chronology. For the general purposes of drama and comedy, however, it is worth remembering that the audience may still be attuned to the linear unfolding of events.

Flashbacks present many technical challenges. They are not easy to structure into the narrative in a convincing way, and they tend to interrupt the flow of the story in the 'here and now' of screen-time. Flashbacks also present the writer with conundrums concerning the logic and content of scenes set in the 'past' in relation to those set in the onscreen 'present'. In some genres however, they provide the writer with exciting opportunities.

If you are grappling with a story outline that seems to require flashbacks or flash-forwards, consider how immediate and dramatic your story might be if the event that affected your protagonist in the past were inserted instead into the current action of the present. Study the following sections to gain more insight into the creative treatment of story chronology.

Deadlines, ticking clocks and high-stakes dilemmas

We have discussed the most immediate challenge for the writer: to structure dramatic highlights into the here and now of 'present' screen-time and to make that 'now' as heightened, exciting or stimulating as possible. One way to achieve this dramatic sense of pacing is to incorporate a deadline.

One common device in a thriller or suspense story is to give the protagonist a deadline or time limit within which to achieve their goals. This technique helps to focus the audience on the main story outcomes and thus creates suspense. For instance, the protagonist must find the killer and defuse a time bomb within three hours, before midnight. This technique creates anxiety in the audience, who are now aware that the problem involves time as well as action. This formula becomes extra potent if the stakes are high enough to make the audience feel worried about the story outcomes. For instance, if the hero fails to stop the villain, the bomb will explode at midnight, destroying an entire city.

This is known as the 'ticking clock' device. Essentially, the writer gives the protagonist a deadline, and puts them under pressure to solve a problem within a narrow time frame. When the 'ticking clock' deadline is married to a high-stakes dilemma (life or death), the writer ensures that the scope and range of the characters' experiences and emotions will be very wide. Everyone on screen generally has a lot to lose, and the feeling becomes more urgent as they can lose the game at any moment.

In this typical suspense scenario—say, a James Bond film—the time of the tale can be tailored to correspond to the time of the telling. In the final act, the hero may only have 30 minutes left to stop the bomb going off. The audience then watches him conduct his search in the 'real time' of 30 minutes in the cinema.

This special combination of chronological elements creates great suspense. As they observe the ticking clock of the time bomb, the audience can identify closely with the expectations and fears of the protagonist. Sharing the protagonist's onscreen time frame, we go through the same highs and lows, the surprises and let-downs, that are known in the film industry as 'a roller-coaster ride'.

So, in the suspense thriller, we see the proof of Aristotle's point about the unities of space and time. In one way, the chronology of the protagonist's 'outer' journey is kept deliberately narrow (a deadline) in order to reflect the large 'inner' psychological changes that are taking place as the character moves to solve a central dramatic problem.

Another well-known example of the high-stakes ticking clock is provided by the entire scenario of Alfred Hitchcock's thriller, *Rope*. This story unfolds in 'real time', such that the time of the tale and the time of the telling are virtually identical. The plot covers the hour and a half it takes a man to murder his friend, hide the body and then host a party at which the body is concealed inside a trunk, which is then used as a casual coffee table during the social gathering.

In the Nick of Time also unfolds in a 'real time' scenario. The protagonist must save his kidnapped daughter before she is killed by terrorists who have also targeted a political figure for assassination. The protagonist is given a 90-minute deadline which coincides perfectly with the time of the telling (screen-time). It is resolved 'in the nick of time', as he saves his daughter and the political candidate all in the space of the 90-minute deadline.

This deadline device is useful for the writer to unify the action that plays out between two or more characters in two or more locations simultaneously. In *In The Nick of Time*, the protagonist must both save his kidnapped daughter and prevent a political assassination. This creates a difficult dilemma for the protagonist, one deadline may interfere with the other. The protagonist's adventure lies in his attempt to achieve two deadlines in two conflicting realms. This dual deadline provides the writer with a classic way to build audience suspense. The deadline puts more pressure on the protagonist, adding more 'heat' to his dramatic problem.

In *Film Art: An introduction*, David Bordwell and Kristin Thompson conduct a thorough examination of classic film structures (Bordwell & Thompson 2001). The authors point out that the deadline can be measured by various orders of time. The writer can use a deadline to put pressure on a protagonist. The deadline can be enforced by calendars (*Around the World in Eighty Days*), by clocks (*High Noon*), by threat ('You've got a week to find the plans or destroy the building . . .'), or simply by cues that time is running out (the ticking clock that indicates a bomb will explode at midnight—can the protagonist save the day?).

In several genres, the climax of a classic film is often involved with the protagonist's deadline. If the protagonist achieves their goal in time, the audience is relieved of suspense; if not, they usually have another trial to go through before the story can close in a way that is satisfying to the audience.

The usefulness of deadline devices reminds us of a key point: the audience is more interested in what happens *next* in the story, rather than in what happened *before*. This means that the writer needs to keep the audience on their tocs—to keep them guessing as to 'What will happen next?' An audience can lose interest in or lose track of the plot if the action depends on episodes that occurred long ago in the protagonist's past. The audience needs to feel in touch with current events onscreen in front of them.

Parallel action

Another classic, reliable and technically 'neat' way of constructing the 'now' is to use parallel action. This means that the writer can cut between two or more characters, each acting in the same 'present' but in different locations. This technique is used to build suspense by transporting the audience from one scenario to the next and back again, making comparisons between the two scenarios. In creating parallel action, the writer often incorporates a deadline or common goal to unify the action that is playing out in both locations simultaneously.

Think of the old silent films that pioneered the technique of parallel action:

Scene 1: Villain ties the heroine to the railway tracks.

Scene 2: In the woods, our hero jumps on his horse, taking off to save her.

Scene 3: Train comes through a tunnel and approaches the squealing victim as the villian escapes.

Scene 4: We cut back to the hero as he races through the woods towards them.

Parallel action keeps the audience ahead of the action and, sometimes, one step ahead of the protagonist. The audience can see the villain, the heroine and the train before the hero can. The deadline? We all know that the train may run over the heroine when it comes through the tunnel. This creates a sense of audience participation in the action and anticipation of the results. Will the hero reach her in time?

Circular or non-linear chronology

As our exposure to new digital and Internet-based technologies increases, we are seeing more innovative and avant-garde treatment of plot, characters and chronology. Writers working in multimedia and Web-based media can create and reflect a radically different set of perceptions and story environments. Our enjoyment of virtual reality, avatars and role-play, interactive movies, chat-rooms and other cyber-based zones is already challenging our awareness and understanding of what 'reality' in the 'here and now' means.

Of course, science fiction has been exploring this realm since the 1960s and 1970s, when films such as *Blade Runner, 2001: A Space Odyssey, Planet of the Apes* and Andrei Tarkovsky's *Solaris* (Solyaris) opened up new dimensions of experiential time and space. *Blade Runner* and *Planet of the Apes* compared the human condition with that of other species (including androids). *2001: A Space Odyssey* and *Solaris* created a universe where present and past merge in a fluid continuum.

Independent film-makers working outside the big studio systems have also pushed the envelope on expression and technique and are often grouped together in the 'art-house' genre.

Non-linear story models have been a staple of art-house films for decades, as film-makers associated with various art movements often ignore or subvert the dictates of classic storytelling.

With their avant-garde 1960s' pastiches, the French 'new wave' director Jean-Luc Godard and American pop artist Andy Warhol defied the linear and logical dictates of Hollywood's 'straight corridor' style. In Godard's *Weekend*, and Warhol's *Chelsea Girls* linear chronology is replaced by a seemingly random chronology of events. This more haphazard treatment of plot and chronology challenges the entire foundation of Western film language, presenting worlds where events happen seemingly at random or within an entirely 'other' universe.

For now, we might examine films such as *Sliding Doors*, *Run Lola Run*, *Short Cuts* or *Pulp Fiction* as popular examples of non-linear story structure, where multiple protagonists and fragmented time frames are the norm.

Run Lola Run puts a new spin on the classic deadline-driven suspense. Written and directed by Tom Tykwer, this screenplay represents the story world as a split prism of three parallel universes. The script has a circular structure that repeats essentially the same scenario and the same characters in each of three repetitive acts. However, in each of these three scenarios, there are crucial differences in the action and outcomes.

The set-up takes up the first ten minutes of the story. Lola talks to her boyfriend Mani on the phone and learns that she must get to him in twenty minutes—he has lost a bag of money belonging to a drug lord and must rob a supermarket in order to replace the cash. After this initial set-up, there are three acts representing not the beginning, middle and end, but three distinctive 'spins' of the story wheel. Each act includes the same set-up, location and characters, and each has totally different pay-offs and outcomes. They are in effect three self-contained stories and yet there are clever links and cross-overs between them.

In act one, Lola fails to get the money and arrives at Mani's side just as he is robbing the supermarket. They are caught by the police and Lola is shot. Act two essentially repeats the key elements of the first scenario. In order to save Mani, Lola steals some money from her father's bank and reaches Mani's side just as he is about to rob the store. Act two ends when Mani is knocked down by an ambulance.

Act three gives us another interpretation of Lola's story. Lola gets the money by gambling at the casino and reaches Mani just as he delivers his own stash to the drug lord. Lola gets away with the money and the boyfriend.

The writer of *Run Lola Run* presents an intriguing structure where the three acts have a symmetry and repetition that is almost mathematical in its consistency. Tom Tykwer sets up a kind of non-linear framework where time is treated in a very fluid way and reconstructed to produce even more surprises for the audience.

Sliding Doors makes clever and unconventional use of chronology by exploring a fantasy dimension of space and time. It explores the life of a young woman as if there were two 'versions' of her character, each inhabiting a simultaneous reality or a parallel universe. This doppelganger theme (the notion of the exact double) is one with a firm foundation in literary and film history—consider the science fiction archetype of *Dr Jekyll and Mr Hyde*.

In her book *The Haunted Screen*, German film theorist Lotte Eisner examines the early German silent film *The Student of Prague* (also known as *The Doppelganger*), which had its roots in opera and was produced in three different film versions, thus becoming a genre unto itself (Eisner 1973). In each of the 1913, 1926 and

1936 versions of this classic split-identity story, we see the early use of special effects—including special lighting and sets, a split screen and super-imposition techniques—to 'double' the actor on the screen and create a visual world of romantic anguish.

The story of a person who has lost their shadow or reflection has many ancient precedents in European legend and opera. Such a complex double universe presents clear challenges for the screenwriter, who must treat the two 'versions' of the protagonist almost as dual protagonists, each with their own plotline.

The writer of *Sliding Doors* engages the rules of this particular story genre by providing several anchors to keep the audience in-step with this complex plot. The story depicts a single woman who is 'split' into two as we follow different versions of her existence. The 'first' protagonist's romantic plotline is intercut with that of the 'second' in the old style of parallel action. The same actress (Gwyneth Paltrow) plays both parts.

In one 'version' of her life, the romantic heroine ditches her old boyfriend and falls in love anew. In the other, parallel story-line, she ends up staying with her original boyfriend. In the main plotline, the protagonist cuts her hair short. In the contrasting subplot, she leaves her hair long. This important visual cue helps the audience to recognise and distinguish between the 'two in one' protagonist as she seems to appear simultaneously in parallel story strands or plotlines within the one time frame.

Sliding Doors is a well-constructed screenplay that observes the rules of the genre and succeeds in challenging the audience by manipulating the rules of a linear, realist framework. Two aspects of the single protagonist exist in the same chronological framework almost as if they were two different people.

The premise of this film suggests that we all create different imaginative 'versions' of ourselves which may be at odds with our everyday reality. However, one problem remains: it is never quite clear to the audience which version of her life is 'real' and which is the 'fantasy' version of her very active imagination.

Such confusions can overwhelm the audience and prevent the central message from getting across. *Jacob's Ladder* is an equally challenging, though less popular, film that dramatises the different aspects of individual psychology. While it is refreshing in its approach to subject matter, *Jacob's Ladder* is an example of how a good story idea can be brought undone by a messy chronology. The plot follows a Vietnam veteran who was a 'guinea pig' in dangerous and top-secret drug experiments organised by shadowy powers in the US government. Writer Bruce Rubin takes us into the mind of an ex-soldier whose present 'reality' is fused into a hallucinogenic mish-mash of past and present.

One problem here is that the story jumps back and forward in time, with too few firm anchor points for the audience to latch on to. Thus, we are never sure when we are in the present and when we are in the past. In setting up this confusing scenario, the writer was perhaps trying to reproduce for the audience the 'altered state' of the protagonist. However, the writer's bet doesn't pay off. An audience may simply not want to feel disoriented by a plot. The protagonist may feel sick and confused, but *we* in the audience don't wish to feel that way. There is a difference between feeling empathy for a character's illness and feeling as sick or frustrated as they do.

When a writer tampers with the audience's sense of chronology, this can affect their appreciation of the plot. The more a writer departs from the conventions of linear narrative, the more care they must take to ensure that the audience actually understands how the story unfolds. If they don't 'get' the story, an audience will simply walk out of the cinema feeling frustrated and hostile and, after *Jacob's Ladder*, slightly dizzy.

In *Pulp Fiction*, the conventions of straight-line chronology are completely and merrily upturned. There is no single protagonist instead, we follow three central male characters—Vincent, Jules and Butch—as they act out their duties in Wallace's crime empire.

The story opens in a restaurant, where two hoodlums are staging a robbery. We then cut to a seemingly unrelated story—the adventures of Vincent, the gangster. We journey with Vincent on a big night out with the boss's wife. Vince and the boss's wife happily win a dance trophy, but then Vince must resuscitate her after she takes a drug overdose.

Act two of *Pulp Fiction* takes us sideways into yet another subplot, that of Butch the boxer. Butch refuses to throw a fight, organised by Vincent's boss, and ends up on the run with a lot of cash. At the end of act two, Butch shoots Vincent, who has come to find him for the boss. In act three, we flash back to the day before the prior action and pick up Vincent's story again, following a completely different story strand.

The story follows Vincent from within a flashback and ends back at the restaurant, where the story began. At this point, the writer repeats some of the action we have seen in the prologue. Only this time, we carry on into the restaurant robbery scene that is cut so short in the start. Vincent and his sidekick Jules are diners in the restaurant. They manage to diffuse the robbery situation and protect the bag they are delivering to the boss.

The final image is of Vincent, walking safe and sound out of the restaurant, going about his business. We know, of course, that he is about to meet his death at any moment, because have seen his death scene in the previous act.

The chronology of the *Pulp Fiction* plot breaks many rules

of linear narrative and challenges the viewer to put the pieces together like a jigsaw. While audiences are often confused by the storyline in *Pulp Fiction*, they go back again and again because the general mood is so exciting and unpredictable. This balance between unpredictable fun and sheer confusion is a fine line for any writer to tread. By examining the cinematic order of space and time you can put a fresh spin on classic conventions and delight the audience.

There is no doubt that great narrative effects can be gained by creating and manipulating multiple time frames and other devices. The writers of *Pulp Fiction*, *Sliding Doors*, *The Matrix* and *Run Lola Run* have each created intrigue and surprise by doing so. Rather than using the straight-line chronology of classic convention, these scripts pause to examine how different characters cope with the same situations at different points along the time/space continuum. This new approach to linear chronology makes such screenplays 'feel' fresh. Certainly they are more challenging for the audience, who must sometimes struggle to put the pieces of a puzzle together.

Get to know the conventions that govern the unfolding of screen chronology and then exploit them or subvert them as you will. At best, you need to make a detailed study of genre and of previous screenplays where such devices work effectively. In short, this kind of advanced plotting technique requires meticulous attention to genre and plot logic, skills that have been developed in the previous chapters.

EXERCISE 5

Genre and chronology

Look carefully at the characters, human problems, themes and 'worlds' that interest you as a storyteller. Make a review of the work that makes up your folio so far—loose notes, character biographies and backstory.

To assist you with pacing and chronology, you might first examine the conventions of the genre in which you are working. Audiences need the signposts of genre to help them 'get the picture'. Do some research and try to gain some insights in the following areas:

a. What is the typical chronology or time frame required of the genre?

b. What is the type of world and the realms often explored in this genre?

c. What types of character feature in this genre?

Your premise governs three acts

In the last chapter we discussed the importance of plot, placing special emphasis on the balance between 'the time of the tale' and the 'time of the telling'. We discovered that plotting begins with decisions about your story chronology. We also examined devices for the manipulation of chronology including montage, location and setting, deadlines and parallel action, flashbacks, exposition, and so on.

Perhaps the hardest task for the writer is to find a good answer to the 'who cares?' question. Often, to provide an answer, you must fabricate a strong system of reasons to support all aspects of the action and the conflict. Events must be set up so that their underlying causes are visible to the audience. The relations between characters, locations and situations must be governed by a rational and credible system of cause and effect. This is all part of the logic of the plot.

This chapter illustrates how your plot can be planned around turning points or plot points. These story milestones can provide the writer with an easy 'road map' to help you organise your plot chronology. But first, we will focus on the most intangible of the four Ps—premise.

Premise reflects the central concept and themes

While planning the outline of your plot, remind yourself what it is you are actually trying to say or examine through your story. This idea is your premise, the underlying concept that is moti- vating you to write. A good writer organises and edits their themes according to a single, governing premise, which acts as a focus for their ideas and themes. The premise sets the tone of the work and provides a clear goal to aim for in writing every scene.

A theme is an idea or image that you may repeat at various intervals during your story. For instance, in *Run Lola Run* the themes include the fragility of love and trust, the awesome power of money, the unreliable father, the redemptive effect of love, the fickle nature of chance, and so on. In this script, the premise seems to suggest that in this universe of infinite possibilities, it is up to each of us to determine the outcomes of the action.

In *Pulp Fiction*, the themes concern the world of crime, greed, anger, drugs, revenge, violence and awakening. The premise is articulated by the gangster Jules at the end of the story. It concerns the individual's ability to shift their moral perspective, depending on their responsibilities and desires. Jules's story illustrates that we may see ourselves as righteous while doing our work; however, if not careful we may finally recognise that we are actually contributing to the evil in the world.

In *Basic Instinct*, themes concern the alluring, seductive and drug-like qualities of violence. The script's premise is discussed by Detective Nick Curran and his lover/suspect, Catherine Trammel. It is about the inability ever to know or really trust those who are caught up in such a web. In such conditions, the hunter can become the prey.

In *The Matrix*, themes include the aggressive nature of the police, the *Alice in Wonderland* journey into another world or dimension, and the fuzzy borders between the 'real' world and the virtual, computer-generated dimension. The script's premise is classic science fiction. It is emblazoned on the film's publicity material: the future will not be user-friendly.

In *Thelma & Louise*, themes focus on the difference between freedom and captivity, the need for females to defend themselves, the psychology of theives and the aggressive nature of the police. The script includes many ideas and images about the importance of friendship and about the 'Wild West' as a place in which to reconstruct one's identity.

The central premise of this script perhaps conveys a message about the need to continue the pursuit of freedom, even if it means violating family codes, breaking the law or, finally, even killing oneself. This classic American premise has been adapted from the Western genre, updated and given a new context. The premise of *Thelma & Louise* puts a new 'spin' on an old theme: it isn't the cowboy who escapes the law and achieves freedom, but two women who need to escape their humdrum domestic lives, even if it means breaking the law. These women would rather die than suffer injustice.

With these examples, we can begin to recognise how the

premise works like a private guideline to help the writer shape every scene. The premise helps them to stay on track, organising plot, protagonist and problem according to a clear vision or definite viewpoint.

How a good premise informs the plot

As the most important and fully articulated theme, your premise helps you to decide which elements of your story are definitely to be included onscreen and which can be left aside. Remember that each idea or image must contribute something specific and meaningful to the whole structure. If it doesn't, it is superfluous and can be eliminated. This means that if a scene doesn't help you to illustrate your key themes, either rework it so that it contributes to your themes or cut it.

The premise is an important force in the creation of a film script. When examining the role of the storyteller, we discussed how the use of myth and archetype comes from the desire to interpret the mystery of life's events and find the meaning of existence. No matter what genre you are working in, your work will include a viewpoint or attitude. This may not be explicitly moral or political or sociocultural in tone, but it is still important to realise that your point of view will eventually shape the way the material is presented and perceived.

Your self-image as a writer will partly determine the tone and quality of your entire screenplay. How do you see yourself in relation to the rest of your culture? According to anthropologists and psychologists, the cinema is a screen onto which we project our collective hopes and dreams. At one level, the writer has the opportunity to reinforce these dreams, to demystify the delusions of the culture, to satirise or lampoon them, or to smash them cynically.

Writers who operate from the starting point that they actually have something to say to an audience will communicate better than those who are merely 'shooting the breeze', 'doodling' or 'spinning a yarn'. A good writer is one who has thought deeply about their subject matter, digested this material, and carefully formulated a viewpoint or attitude to share with the audience. This viewpoint need not be stated in a blunt, obvious way; rather, it should be evident in the actions and attitudes of the characters. The premise is an invisible structure, but it will still permeate the tone of the work.

This doesn't mean that you must have an agenda to push, but it does mean that you should be trying to tell us something we may not already know or to put a fresh 'spin' on a classic idea. You don't need to preach to the audience. You do, however, need to think carefully about the full implications of your story.

In his important text *The Art of Dramatic Writing*, Lajos Egri examines the premise as the unifying force of any theatrical play. He points out that the premise contains essential clues about character, conflict and resolution. It acts as the driving force that helps a writer to plan out their story in order to achieve a basic emotional result with the audience.

Egri examines several of Shakespeare's plays and their premises. He points out that *Romeo and Juliet* begins with a deadly feud between two families and ends with tragedy for the son and daughter of each. 'Romeo, believing Juliet really dead, drinks poison and dies beside her. When Juliet awakens and finds Romeo dead, without hesitation she decides to unite with him in death.'

Egri carefully traces the logic of Shakespeare's plot to conclude:

125

[T]his play obviously deals with love. But there are many kinds of love. No doubt this was a great love, since the two lovers not only defied family tradition and hate, but threw away life to unite in death. The premise then, as we see it is: 'great love defies even death.' (Egri 1960, p. 3).

On the great play *Ghosts*, by Ibsen, Egri concludes:

the basic idea is heredity. The play grew out of a Biblical quotation which is the premise: 'The sins of the fathers are visited on the children.' Every word uttered, every move made, every conflict in the play, comes about because of this premise. (Egri 1960, p. 6).

According to Egri, 'every good play must have a well-formulated premise. There may be more than one way to phrase the premise, but, however it is phrased, the thought must be the same.' (Egri 1960, p. 6).

This all suggests that the writer has a particular responsibility: to really think about their material and offer some piece of wisdom to the audience.

Playwrights usually get an idea, or are struck by an unusual situation, and decide to write a play around it. The question is whether that idea, or that situation, provides sufficient basis for a play . . . No idea, and no situation, was ever strong enough to carry you through to its logical conclusion without a clear-cut premise. (Egri 1960, p. 6).

Egri warns that without a premise, the writer gets lost.

You may modify, elaborate, vary your original idea or situation, or even lead yourself into another situation, but you will not know where you are going. You will flounder, rack your brain to invent further situations to round out your play. You may find these situations—and you will still be without a play. You must have a premise—a premise which will lead you unmistakably to the goal your play hopes to reach. (Egri 1960, p. 6).

Egri advises that the writer can arrive at a premise in a great many ways.

You may start with an idea which you at once convert to a premise, or you may develop a situation first and see that is has potentialities which need only the right premise to give them meaning and suggest an end. (Egri 1960, p. 6).

He also points out that while no premise is necessarily a universal truth, the writer needs to assume the convinction that their premise *is true*.

Poverty doesn't always lead to crime, but if you've chosen this premise, it does in your case. The same principle governs all premises. The premise is the conception, the beginning of a play. The premise is a seed and it grows into a plant that was contained in the original seed . . . (Egri 1960, p. 29).

How to identify your premise

Remember that the best writing comes from passion—'the fire in the belly.' Ask yourself the following questions about your role as storyteller:

- What really makes you passionate as a human being?
- What makes you particularly angry?
- What do you wish to convey to the audience about the larger moral/political/sociocultural questions of life?
- What intelligent conclusions have you drawn about human nature that may interest an audience?

- How can you use your protagonist, problem and plot to illustrate your viewpoint?

No doubt you have plenty to say about these questions. As you begin to write and organise your complex ideas, consider carefully your premise and your themes.

Try to list the themes that concern you in your story; jot them down loosely in your folio. Then organise your themes in a kind of pyramid structure, with the most important themes at the top (see figure 2.1). The premise will sit at the pinnacle of your pyramid as a central concept. Use it to help you focus on the other themes.

The three-act structure

In recent years, writers have begun to identify various patterns and paradigms in the structure of the three-act screenplay. Linda Seger points out that 'whether it's a Greek tragedy, a five-act Shakespearean play, a four-act dramatic series, or a seven-act movie-of-the-week, we still see the basic three-act structure: beginning, middle, and end—or set-up, development, and resolution'. (Seger 1994, p. 20).

Seger looks at the way a feature film is usually broken down to include a ten- to fifteen-page set-up of the story followed by about twenty more pages of development in act one. The long second act might run to 45–60 pages, followed by a fairly fast-paced third act of 25–30 pages.

In his influential text *The Screenwriter's Workbook*, Syd Field also provides a simple paradigm for the basic three-act structure. Field describes this basic structure as a tool which helps the writer shape the screenplay with maximum dramatic effect. (Field 1984, p. 17).

One aim of the screenwriter is to manage the complex plotting requirements of the protagonist's arc or journey as it unfolds over time. One way of achieving this is to arrange the story within a classic three-act structure, where each act represents the beginning, middle and end of the protagonist's story. These three acts represent the largest structure of the screenplay; the basic outline of the main plot. Within this outline, you can organise the chronology or time frame of the plot.

The purpose of each act is clear and simple. In act one, the writer establishes a protagonist and a world; then they create a disturbance or problem within that world. In act two, this problem leads to further conflict, complications and struggle. Finally, in act three, the protagonist acts to resolve the problem that was established back in act one. *The protagonist must be seen to change as a result of the action over three acts.*

In previous exercises, you selected episodes or events that keep the audience tuned-in and interested in the arc of the protagonist. The following situations may be thought of as important plot points for the protagonist to deal with:

- complications
- conflicts
- challenges
- barriers to a goal
- reversals of fortune.

These screen events, or plot points, will drive the action right from the start of act one, through the middle act, to a rousing climax and conclusion at around page 100. From now on, we will refer to these plot points as turning points.

How to organise turning points

The screenplay's three acts can be mapped according to a simple formula that has evolved from theatrical conventions into a cornerstone of most mainstream film technique, regardless of genre.

The term 'turning point' is part of general industry terminology and is a useful tool for writers working in most genres. In order to keep moving forward, your story must be driven by major conflicts, problems or turning points—events that occur at regular intervals throughout the three acts. These turning points punctuate the story and help to organise and order your plot chronology—the protagonist's journey and that of the audience, who must stay interested in the outcomes from start to finish.

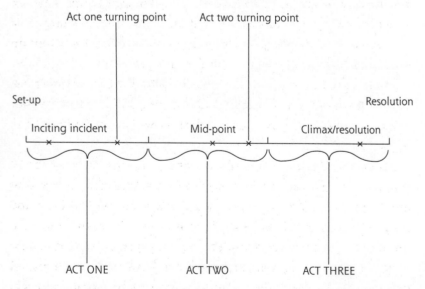

Figure 6.1   Three-act structure

In general, we may imagine that there are three turning points, which occur at the end of each act, as well as two crucial support points known as the inciting incident and the mid-point, which come at the beginning and in the middle of the script. In addition, there are two more areas of the script which need to be considered. These work like book-ends, holding up the entire story: the set-up and the resolution. These seven key points are illustrated again in figure 6.1.

The pacing of the story should be set up very early in act one so as to win strong and immediate audience approval and fascination. The inciting incident, or catalyst, acts as a hook to lure the audience into the plot by disturbing the 'normal' world of the early set-up. This inciting incident gets the ball rolling on the action and reveals the protagonist's main problem.

The next main point of interest occurs at the end of the first act, usually at around pages 25–30 of a 100-page script. The act one turning point is often the location of the crucial murder, of lovemaking, or of a disaster that grabs the audience's attention and helps to drive the action with fresh intrigue.

The writer then builds on this early interest by moving the protagonist swiftly through the mid-section of the script, known as act two, where their initial dilemma will be built upon and embellished.

Traditionally, act two is the writer's danger zone. At 45 or 50 minutes into the action, the writer must maintain the momentum and focus of the first act, otherwise the audience will feel lost and may switch off or fall asleep. The writer must keep the audience on the edge of their seats by drawing the protagonist further into a web of intrigue, complications and overwhelming problems, all of which make the audience reflect upon the dilemma and feel anxious about the progress of the protagonist's journey. This anxiety is a desirable function of suspense: the audience waits with baited breath to know the outcomes.

In general, the writer achieves this aim at the mid-point, which represents the protagonist's lowest point. Here they seem to have failed: they have been captured by the enemy or have lost their love, their job, their apartment or their money. This is the pit of despair. How can they survive?

Christopher Vogler points out that the second half of act two is often the time when the heroic protagonist shows their true spirit and determination. At this point, the protagonist will 'seize the sword' that symbolises their ability to look danger in the face and bravely tackle their problem. Despite the terrible odds against them at the mid-point, the rest of act two is about showing the protagonist get up and 'get back on their horse' and ride towards the ultimate conflict—the climax.

In act three, the writer leads the protagonist towards the final confrontation, the grand conflict at the end of act three, known as the 'climax'. This section of the screenplay shows clearly how the protagonist solves (or partly solves) their main problem. The final section of the screenplay must also indicate how a change has occurred in the protagonist.

The story finishes with a resolution, the last few minutes of the film, which indicates the protagonist's emotional and situational response to the climax. The resolution represents the moment where the protagonist's arc comes to rest.

In the end, we see how the inciting incident, and the dramatic problem that it initiates, must add up to a seemingly inevitable string of events. The writer must lead the protagonist (and the audience) towards a stirring conclusion. The protagonist's problems aren't necessarily solved, but they are at least resolved or dealt with in a manner that the audience will believe and feel satisfied by. All the main questions about plot and character should have been resolved by this end-point.

The resolution will reflect back on the set-up by showing how much the protagonist has changed during the course of the action. The resolution will generally 'prove', or confirm, the writer's premise. For instance, in *Thelma & Louise*, the two heroines drive off a cliff rather than face capture by the police. This confirms the premise that it is better to keep running—even into death—rather than submit to injustice.

Let us now revise the seven main structural plot points, or turning points. Remember, your premise should inform your selection of events.

1 The set-up

This sequence of scenes situates your character within settings and locations that help to ground your premise. Usually over the first five to seven scenes, the protagonist's world is set up. This world represents the 'status quo', or 'situation normal', for the protagonist and their world. We are introduced to their main strengths, weaknesses, beliefs, cultural and social influences—and their desires—*before* the catalysing moment which will rock the foundation of that world.

2 The inciting incident

This scene identifies the first event of excitement and/or anguish which motivates the protagonist and *hooks the audience into the story*. It leads to decisions that, in turn, lead to further turning points. Syd Field calls this the 'inciting incident', while Lynda Seger calls it the 'catalyst'. This first incident in the story generally occurs at around pages 10–15 (or around 10–15 minutes into the story) and gets the story going with an exciting 'bang'. The protagonist's problem may be established by the inciting incident and further reinforced or complicated by the next turning point.

3 Act one turning point

This is the point of no return: after this action or event, the protagonist's world will never again be the same. Some dramatic action (usually based on issues of survival, bonding or achievement) propels the protagonist into a new world or way of being, and helps to drive the action. This occurs at the end of the first act, usually at around pages 25–30 of a 100-page script.

4 The mid-point

This is the lowest ebb of the protagonist's journey, the point where they are most down on their luck and in trouble. In the Syd Field model, the second act contains two important turning points. The turning point that falls halfway through the plot is known as the mid-point. This point corresponds roughly to the actual mid-point in the screenplay (around page 50) and thus helps the writer to structure the two halves of their work. The first half moves the protagonist to the depths of danger and despair; the second half forces the protagonist to take control of their circumstance.

5 The act two turning point

Here, the protagonist struggles to overcome all the odds and to climb back out of the pit of despair. The act two turning point falls at the end of act two and helps to build towards the climax. The turning point must crystallise the protagonist's main conflict or problem. In the second part of act two, the writer must steer the protagonist through sticky situations and back on the course of their journey. Field suggests that the turning point at the end of act two often consists of a major confrontation between the protagonist and a key support character (whether a love interest or an antagonist). This moment will redirect the protagonist on a rapid path towards the action of the climax.

6 The climax

The act three turning point, towards the end of act three, represents the climax of the story. All the story elements come into conflict at this point and test the mettle of the protagonist. This is the grand finale and should have just as much impact on the protagonist (and the audience) as the first plot point. It usually brings all the strands of action and subplot into play so that the hero *must* deal with the problem in a situation of direct and major conflict. The climax should prove the author's premise.

7 The resolution or denouement

This describes the few minutes of screen-time that occur after the final climax or plot point at the end of act three. This last interval provides an opportunity for the writer and the protagonist to show the audience how they have resolved their emotional and situational response to the key dramatic problem. The resolution also gives some indication of the protagonist's future direction.

Here are some examples of premise and plot points from well-known films. In chapter 10 you can begin to make your own outlines based on this scheme.

Sunset Boulevard

Screenplay by Billy Wylder, Charles Brackett and G. Marshman

Premise?

Sometimes a woman will kill a man if she can't have him to herself. Or, There is nothing tragic about being 50, unless you are trying to be 25.

Set-up

A young man is found by the press and police floating dead in the pool of a wealthy, former movie star. We flash back to the same man, Joe Gillis, as a penniless writer who is behind in his car payments.

Inciting incident

15 minutes

While fleeing the repossession agents who are after his car, Joe stumbles into the derelict mansion of Norma Desmond, who employs him on the spot to edit her epic screenplay about Salome.

Act one plot point

35 minutes

After Max, the butler, sends the repossession agents away from the mansion, Joe accepts Norma's offer to live at her mansion and her lavish gifts of clothing.

Mid-point

50 minutes

Joe tries to leave Norma's mansion after meeting his writer friend Betty and discussing a script idea, but returns when he learns that Norma has slashed her wrists.

Act two plot point

1 hour, 25 minutes

Joe and Betty kiss while working on their secret screenplay project, but when Joe goes home, he finds Norma on the phone to Betty, telling her that he's a gigolo.

Climax

1 hour, 38 minutes

When Joe starts packing to leave the mansion, Norma threatens to shoot herself, but shoots him instead.

Resolution

1 hour 42 minutes

Joe floats dead in the pool as Norma poses for press cameras, which she thinks are movie cameras set to capture her performance in her latest film, *Salome*.

Thelma & Louise

Screenplay by Callie Khouri

Premise?

It's better to die free than to spend your life in prison.

- Note dual protagonists who share the focus of our attention.
- Note the happy, upbeat interlude at the mid-point; a common structure in stories that have a tragic ending.
- Note how the happy interlude at the mid-point is neatly reversed when the women discover that their money has been stolen by Thelma's new boyfriend.

Set-up

A hard-working waitress, Louise, and her best friend Thelma, a frustrated housewife, decide to skip their small, humdrum, Mid-Western American lives for a girls' weekend alone.

Inciting incident

20 minutes

The women drive to a roadside bar where Louise shoots a guy who is trying to rape Thelma.

Act one plot point

28 minutes

With the cops on their trail, the women decide to stay on the road and Louise calls her boyfriend asking him to send cash.

Mid-point

1 hour

At an isolated motel, Louise is briefly reunited with her boyfriend, while Thelma makes love with a handsome hitchhiker who ends up robbing them of all their cash.

Act two plot point

1 hour, 32 minutes

Thelma and Louise hit the road to Mexico but are pulled over by a cop whom they overpower and lock up in the trunk of his car. This makes them federal criminals—wanted dead or alive.

Climax

1 hour, 50 minutes

The women are chased across country by police who force their old T-Bird right up against the edge of a deep canyon.

Resolution

1 hour, 59 minutes

Rather than surrender to the police, the two women decide to drive right off the canyon's edge into the blue beyond.

Basic Instinct

Screenplay by Joe Eszterhas

Premise?

Sometimes when the evidence gets complicated, a cop has to trust his instincts. But then again, he might be wrong, especially if he is in love with his number one suspect.

- Note that this script is stacked densely with turning points that keep the audience guessing and asking more questions. It exemplifies the mystery suspense genre where the writer is under pressure to keep providing the audience with fresh information and clues to help figure out 'who dunnit'.

Set-up

When a former rock star and heavy cocaine user is killed by a beautiful blonde with an ice pick, Detective Nick Curran—bad boy of San Francisco's homicide squad—is called in to investigate.

Inciting incident

10 minutes

Nick investigates the dead man's girlfriend, Catherine Trammel, a writer of murder mysteries, and her best friend, Roxy. Both women are blonde.

Act one plot point

30 minutes

After Catherine passes a lie detector test in which she denies killing her boyfriend, Nick drives her home, takes his first drink of alcohol in three months and then has a fight with his ex-girlfriend and police psychologist, Beth.

Mid-point

1 hour

When Nick's enemy, an Internal Affairs inspector, is killed by an unknown assassin, Nick is suspended from duty. He believes that Catherine did the shooting.

Act two plot point

1 hour, 15 minutes

After making passionate love with Catherine, Nick tells her that he will convict her of murder. He then feels confused when he learns that his ex-girlfriend, Beth, has a shadowy past that includes a college-days obsession with Catherine and a marriage that ended in an unsolved murder.

Climax

1 hour, 50 minutes

Nick's partner and buddy is murdered, seemingly by Beth, who arrives on the scene to be shot dead by Nick.

Resolution

1 hour, 53 minutes

Nick goes home to find Catherine waiting for him, so they make love. But there is an ice pick under the bed. Will she use it?

Psycho

Screenplay by Joseph Stefano from a novel by Robert Bloch

Premise?

Guilt and repression can affect the mind so powerfully that we can convince ourselves we are actually someone else and thus remain free of responsibility.

- Note the long act one set-up of Marion Crane and Norman Bates.
- Note the unconventional death of the protagonist at 46 minutes into the action. Then Norman Bates takes over as our focus of interest.

Set-up

Marion Crane makes love with Sam, a divorced man with few prospects, in a cheap hotel before going to her job at a real estate office.

Inciting incident

12 minutes

Marion steals $40 000 from her boss's office and leaves town in a hurry.

Act one plot point

46 minutes

Marion is knifed to death by Norman Bates, proprietor of the eerie roadside motel where she takes shelter while running from the law.

Mid-point

1 hour, 15 minutes

A private investigator, hired by Marion's boss to find the money, suspects Norman Bates but is knifed to death by Norman's 'mother' who appears as a crazy, jealous old woman.

Act two plot point

1 hour, 24 minutes

When Marion's sister, Lila, and Sam show up to look for Marion, we see Norman talk to his 'mother' and hide her in the basement of their decrepit mansion.

Climax

1 hour, 42 minutes

With Sam lying injured, Lila searches the Bates mansion alone and wanders into the basement where Norman attacks her with a knife, dressed as his dead mother.

Resolution

1 hour, 45 minutes

While Norman sits in jail, wrapped in a blanket, the police psychologist explains that the young man has been overcome by a severe personality disorder in which he believes he actually *is* his mother—the 'woman' who killed Marion and the detective—the woman he actually murdered as a child many years before.

EXERCISE 6

Premise and protagonist psychology

What is driving your protagonist may also be driving you. Their central problem may reflect your own concerns in life. Use your exploration of character to clarify these ideas as you work through the turning points that will structure your story.

6.1 Review the 'who cares?' question by considering your premise carefully.

- Just what is the relevance of your story to the larger culture represented by a wide audience?
- What attracted you to tell it in the first place?
- What feelings or thoughts do you want to leave the audience with?

6.2 Review your list of scenes, sequences and events.

- How can your choice of events and conflicts help to illuminate your premise?
- How might character action and reaction crystallise the themes and concepts you want to explore as a writer?

6.3 Identify which of your scenes are potential plot points according to the following questions:

Questions about the set up

- Does your choice of location, setting and events help to establish your character's psychology?

Questions about the inciting incident

- Does the inciting incident result from conflicts between different characters/different realms/different goals and values in the protagonist's inner and outer worlds?
- How do these add up to a specific dramatic problem and move the protagonist towards change?

Questions about your act one turning point

- How does your choice of events affect your protagonist?
- What basic human needs are in jeopardy?

Questions about your mid-point

- Does your selection of events put the protagonist in a situation where they must question everything and doubt some inner aspect of self?
- How does the mid-point follow on from the earlier turning points?

Questions about your act two turning point

- What major confrontation does your protagonist engage in at this point?
- With which key support characters?
- Does it move your protagonist towards the search for a new solution?

Questions about your climax

- Does the climax bring together the key characters and forces that the protagonist has been struggling with?
- Does the climax bring together the key structural elements the writer is grappling with? Plot? Premise? Protagonist and dramatic problem?
- Does the protagonist clearly solve or partly solve their dramatic problem?

Questions about your resolution

- Will the audience feel satisfied that the protagonist's key problems have been dealt with and resolved?
- Look back at your first and second turning points. How has the protagonist changed during the course of the story?
- Does your resolution provide a sense of the protagonist's future direction?

Scene construction

W e have so far established the premise as the foundation underlying the writer's choice of protagonist, dramatic problem and plot. We have also observed how the three-act structure provides a roadmap for the protagonist's emotional journey comprising key turning points. Now it is time to write some of these scenes. In this chapter, we analyse the elements of scene construction, with an aim to create stirring, logical and convincing story material.

Scene structure

In order to reinforce the shape and force of the protagonist's arc, each new scene must tell us something *more* about the way the protagonist is handling their dramatic problem. Information should be built into every scene, for the purpose of advancing the story with a forward momentum. In fact, if a scene doesn't advance the plot, it is not essential to the structure and may well be cut.

There are four simple ways to ensure that the audience gathers more intelligence at every turn:

- In each and every scene, you need to identify both its high point and its purpose.
- In general, there should be new information (set-ups, revelations, obstacles, pay-offs) in each scene so that the story continues to move forward.
- Each scene should reveal something about the protagonist's conflicts, both internal and external.
- Aim to create the highest point of the drama without too much concern for details that can clutter the crucial moments.

The purpose of a scene is usually to provide story exposition to convey information about the plot. Your scenes will be focused around your characters, their conflicts, their world, and their back-story. With all this material to convey, how is a writer to give priority to information that is revealed during the course of three acts?

If a scene reveals nothing new about the protagonist's struggle or journey, there is no structural need to include it.

Ensure that your scenes remain focused on the main plot-lines that emerge from your four Ps.

Screen theorist Robert McKee discusses the way in which scenes are built around an important element of dramatic structure, the beat. McKee describes the beat as an element akin to a turning point. The beat describes 'an exchange of behavior in action/reaction. Beat by beat the changing behaviors shape the turning of a scene.' (McKee 1997, p. 37).

McKee points out that each scene must be constructed as a 'story event' in which there is a degree of perceptible change in the condition of a character's life. To achieve this sense of change, he suggests that a screenwriter look closely at each scene they've written and try to work every scene from beginning to end by 'turning a value at stake in a character's life from positive to the negative or the negative to the positive.' (McKee 1997, p. 36).

In addition, McKee suggests that you ask yourself the following questions about each scene:

- What value is at stake in my character's life at this moment? Love? Truth? Freedom? What?
- How is that value indicated or charged at the top or beginning of the scene? Positive? Negative? Some of both? Make a note of this. Next, turn to the close of the scene and ask:
- Where is this value now? Positive? Negative? Both? Make a note and compare.

McKee suggests that if the answer you give at the end of a scene is the same as one you gave at the opening of the scene, the condition of the protagonist's problem stays unchanged. This means that nothing meaningful happens in the scene; it is a nonevent. As McKee points out, you now have another important question to ask: 'Why is this scene in my script?' If the condition of the protagonist's problem stays unchanged from one end of the scene to the other this suggests that nothing meaningful happens. As McKee points out, it is a nonevent. (McKee 1997, p. 258).

McKee points out that such a scene may be there to provide story exposition to convey information about characters, world, or history to the eavesdropping audience. We have already discussed that if a scene reveals nothing new about the protagonist's struggle or journey, there is no structural need to include it. McKee suggests that 'if exposition is a scene's sole justification, a disciplined writer will trash it and weave its information into the film elsewhere.' (McKee 1997, p. 217).

Each scene stands for the whole

Any scene picked at random from your screenplay can be read as a kind of sample or miniature, scaled-down version of the entire screenplay. That's because each scene will reflect the larger tone, mood, and premise and themes of the screenplay. Each will also reflect certain key elements of the writer's overall plan—the plot, problem and protagonist.

Each scene should fit with what has gone before it and suggest future developments that spark our curiosity. If you read a single scene as an isolated fragment, we should feel curious—compelled to watch it and to stay tuned-in to see what follows. In each new scene, both dialogue and visual cues (action and gesture) must reveal more than we knew before about a character's desires and fears.

Each scene should have enough internal logic and clarity to stand up to scrutiny on its own. This means that you will treat each scene as a self-contained entity, like an individual performance, with its own beginning, middle and end. At the same time, each scene is a link in the continuous chain of cause-and-effect that leads from start to finish.

Cut to the chase

The high point of each scene is the most dramatic moment where key information is revealed. It may also be the moment of conflict between characters in the scene. Your job is to get to this high point as quickly as possible and to focus on how the scene serves the larger purpose of the plot. Don't be distracted by too much set-up along the way. Too much exposition results in a sluggish pace.

When writing scenes, try to focus on the purpose of each scene in relation to the larger narrative goals.

Enter the scene just moments before a high point in the action. If the aim of a scene is to show conflict, don't spend too much time setting up your action. Enter that scene just a few moments before the spark flies that will incite the argument or conflict.

Don't waste time showing two characters who already know each other going through motions that don't convey meaning. There is no point showing the protagonist and her boyfriend before the key action. We don't need to see them meeting in the park, shaking hands and saying hello. Nor do you need to show them arriving at the next location, a café, walking in the door, taking off their coats, sitting down and having a cup of tea. Just cut quickly to each new location and reveal the action near its peak.

For instance, you might put the two characters chatting together, already in the park, then cut straight to the café where they are still chatting about something of direct relevance to the premise or the plot. They may be engaged in the same conversation as in the previous scene, but simply be situated in a new location.

In this way, the writer eliminates trivial or meaningless onscreen business while focusing audience attention on the most relevant details of the plot. By keeping the action rolling forward, the writer can also emphasise the passage of time and stimulate the audience with diverse locations.

Clarify and repeat key details

Some information must be repeated occasionally from scene to scene, especially if it is required for comedic or dramatic effect. You may want to create a 'running gag' by repeating certain images or lines at intervals during the three acts so that the audience understands that some quirky thing happens to the protagonist on a regular basis.

For instance, in *Thelma & Louise*, the women are repeatedly insulted by a red-neck truck driver who makes lewd gestures at them from his truck cabin. This happens once in each act until, in act three, the joke is paid off. The women manage to pull the truck driver over and actually blow up his truck when he refuses to apologise for his repeatedly disgusting antics.

The sight gag is an opportunity to reinforce your dramatic themes and premise. In this example, the two women's audacity not only produces a laugh, but it also foreshadows their dramatic gesture in the climax and supports a central theme of the screenplay: the women's fearless insistence on standing up for themselves despite the consequences.

The need for repetition

Some redundancy or repetition may be required to enforce details that are crucial to our understanding of the plot. Say you are writing a suspense thriller. In act one, you may need to establish the deadline that will drive the entire plot to its conclusion. You may help the audience along with a simple story device. For instance, in an action/adventure story, your audience may need to know that the hero must defuse the bomb by 3 p.m. on Friday or the airport will blow up.

Such *crucial details may need to be conveyed two, or even three, times.* This ensures that the audience does not miss the key information that will drive the protagonist and shape their problem. In such cases, the writer may need to avoid blunt repetition by providing the same information in different ways, using both verbal and visual clues. The classic solution would be to include the image of a ticking clock, or to provide text and dialogue to repeat the important 'set-up' details of your story device.

In *Run Lola Run*, it is clearly established that the protagonist has only twenty minutes to find her boyfriend, Mani. If she cannot find him in time he may commit armed robbery or be killed by his drug dealer boss. This deadline drives the story and is referred to several times in the crucial phone conversation between Lola and Mani that opens act one. Information about the deadline is later reinforced in dialogue and in images of a ticking clock which create suspense.

It is vital to ensure that the audience understands the ins-and-outs of story devices such as the flashback or the deadline. Make sure that you provide them with all the key details that add up to a concise picture of the protagonist's problem or dilemma. Repeat or reiterate these details using visual, aural and verbal cues to make sure the audience is kept on track.

Each scene builds your premise

Despite all your hard work, you will inevitably reach a stage in the work where you may simply lose track of your own story. The writer may occasionally (especially after many days of hard work) lose a sense of what must happen or be said next. At this point, ask yourself three questions to help you decide on a proper course of action for the characters:

- What is my premise?
- What am I trying to prove here?
- What is the purpose of this scene?

In *Thelma & Louise*, the writer maintains a sense of the chase by referring in nearly every scene to the women's dilemma: how to escape, how to reach the next destination, how to engineer their way to freedom. As the police draw ever closer, it becomes clear that the women's options are reduced to two: jail or death. The premise here belongs to the classic Western genre and concerns freedom at all costs. By the end of act three, we realise that this premise includes the idea that the dual protagonists will protect their freedom even at the price of death.

When editing your work, you need to be disciplined. Any scene which adds nothing to the forward movement of the story should be cut. Don't hang on to a scene that's going nowhere. No matter how much you love the lines or the flavour, if it is not contributing to the whole, it is an empty scene.

Treat your dialogue according to the same approach. When writing dialogue, forget 'small talk' unless it contributes something to our understanding of your plot. Dialogue should all be tailored to increase our comprehension of the protagonist, the problem and the premise. If your lines don't fulfil these needs, cut them out and save them for your sequel. It's often hard to eliminate scenes that have taken energy to create, but a good writer won't let ego or sentiment get in the way of a necessary cut. Your motto at such times must be tough: *Kill those darlings!*

Your screenplay isn't a novel

Unlike the screenwriter, who is limited to a mere 100 or so pages, the novelist has unlimited words with which to describe images, feelings and psychological processes of character. The screenplay, however, doesn't include such elaborate descriptions of action or psychology. The screenwriter simply *reports* on the characters' dialogue, actions and locations.

The screenwriter does not have the same narrative 'space' as the novelist, who can devote pages to describing the colour of the sky or the feeling of a kiss. The screenwriter must treat their text like a telegram or haiku poem, with careful juxtaposition of a few handpicked details, each conveying a wealth of symbolic and allegorical meaning.

Avoid the temptation to use stage directions as a way of telling the reader how a character is feeling. This should be made apparent to the audience in dialogue, action and other visible aspects of the drama. The writer's job is to ensure that the protagonist's situation will convey information about their state of mind. The next chapter will deal with these aspects of characterisation in some detail.

EXERCISE 7

Scene construction

7.1 Identify three key turning point scenes and write them in full.

* Construct the scene opening or set-up, the character action, the build-up of tension and the pay-off.
* Be sure to focus on the purpose or intention of the scene and explore how you can layer information which either pays off or sets up some future action.
* Design your scenes around beats of action and reaction, constantly shifting the story values from positive to negative, or negative to positive, and raising or paying off the stakes.
* Pay special attention to the way characters are introduced and to the flow of stage directions and dialogue.
* Cut back or eliminate information that is irrelevant to the main plot.
* Clarify or repeat information that is crucial to the main plot.

7.2 Choose a key scene from your own screenplay and identify the beats, or shifts of mood and value, that occur within the scene. Include the following information in your notes:

* Describe the scene in one sentence.
* State where it fits in the overall plan of the three acts—e.g., is it a turning point?
* Identify the number of beats, or action/reaction shifts.
* Describe each beat, or movement, of the scene as it relates to the protagonist's plotline and to the premise: love/hate, certainty/uncertainty, fear/courage, and so on.

8

Dialogue and characterisation

In the last chapter, we focused on the construction of scene elements, including the set-ups, revelations, conflicts and pay-offs that keep the story moving forward. We now examine the creative writing concerned with characterisation, stage directions and dialogue.

Characterisation

Rather than provide rambling, lengthy descriptions of a character in stage directions, a good screenwriter will indicate character in stealthy ways, using several levels of the script.

A character's motives will be revealed through their values, attitudes and needs—all of which are invisible, abstract qualities. The writer has several vehicles for making these motives visible

157

and concrete. One of the crucial aims is to develop your dialogue as a response to the needs of each character and to the general aims of the plot.

- Dialogue and action are the most important narrative signposts and provide central clues about character.
- Other visual cues (gestures, wardrobe, props) are also useful indicators of character.
- The physical details which define a character may also represent psychological elements of the character and should be carefully chosen for their significance.
- Location, settings, sound effects, action, music and art direction contribute to character, reflecting aspects of personality and backstory which may otherwise be hard to capture in dialogue or action. (These qualities are often beyond the writer's direct control but may be accounted for briefly in good stage directions.)

Stage directions

Unlike the novelist, who can explain to the reader what is going on inside a character's psyche, all the screenwriter has to work with are the actions, words and environment of the character. Apart from dialogue, the stage directions are the place where this information may be coded into the screenplay.

The first stage direction, 'slug line' or 'header' is used to denote the general time of day/night and the location, whether interior or exterior. For example: *Ext. Schoolyard. Day*. The stage directions following the header are used to direct the action of the players. Stage directions (apart from the scene header) are written in prose form and are found at the head of the scene or may be included in the middle of a scene to help punctuate or pace the action. Brief directions to the actors may also be bracketed in the midst of dialogue to give characters particular gestures or tone. For example:

Tony

I can't see a thing.

Either I'm blind or this

map is useless! (rips map into pieces)

Stage directions describe the actions that help a character come to life. Physical habits, peculiarities, special skills, disabilities or injuries can be used like emblems or labels that help the audience to identify the nature or psychology of a character.

For instance, you may decide that your protagonist develops a limp as a way to reflect their outer and inner pain and to complicate their journey. You may emphasise this detail in the stage directions and try to include some 'business' for the actor to perform to show us how the limp affects them in an everyday scenario. Use this visual 'business' or action to complicate the action and to reflect your key themes as an integral part of the story.

Stage directions must also incorporate the key props that help actors to move the action forward. In the following scenes from *Breakfast at Tiffany's*, Paul is meeting the husband of his love interest, Holly, and learning about her past. The key props here are a snapshot of Holly and her children, some coffee cups and a dime.

Example of scripted scene from Breakfast at Tiffany's

EXT. THE TABLE—(LATE AFTERNOON)

Paul continues to study the snapshot. Then he looks up amazed.

> Paul
>
> You're Holly's _father?_

> Doc
>
> Her name's not Holly. She was
> Lulumae Barnes. Was . . . til' she
> Married me. I'm her husband . . .
> Doc Golightly. I'm a horse doctor.
> Animal man. Do some farming too.
> Near Tulip, Texas.

Paul laughs but it is a nervous laugh without humour.

> Doc
>
> This here's no humorous matter son.
> Her brother Fred's getting out of
> The army soon. Lulumae
> Belongs home with her husband,
> her brother and her churren . . .

> Paul
>
> _Children?_

> Doc
> (indicating the snapshot)
>
> Them's her churren...

Paul sits for a moment, staring wide-eyed at Doc. Neither has made the slightest move to touch his coffee. Finally Paul indicates the full coffee cups.

                              Paul
   Finished?

                              Doc
   Yeah.

                              Paul
   Me too. Let's take a little walk.

They rise. Doc takes a change purse out of another pocket, snaps it open, finds a dime and leaves it on the table as a tip. He puts the purse back in his pocket and they move off.

In this scene, each prop has crucial significance. The photo of the young Holly and her children represents her backstory. The photo represents the life of the young woman as a girl who was made to marry young and adopt a brood of children that weren't her own. The photo of the ragged child/woman, surrounded by her children, stands in direct contrast with the image we have of Holly in the current action—that of a well-dressed young sophisticate.

The coffee cups represent the ritual that Doc and Paul, Holly's two men friends, share together as they discuss her. The cups represent the time the two have spent together before we enter the scene. The dime represents Doc's poverty. He keeps the dime carefully within not one, but two, wallets and leaves the single coin carefully as though to give away a precious dime is not done lightly.

Costume

Consider costume as another key element of visual characterisation. Costume elements can 'speak' about a character's purpose or reveal aspects of their backstory. Be careful not to overload the script with excessive details about costume or appearance. For instance, if the colour of a character's hair isn't significant to the role or the action, there is no need to specify it. The producer, casting director and director often prefer to form their own vision of what a character may look like.

Examples of stage directions regarding character, costume and appearance

The introduction of each new character is best done with brief, sharply drawn mini-portraits. These are incorporated in the stage directions when we first meet a character.

In *Breakfast at Tiffany's*, we are introduced to Doc Golightly, Holly's former husband, with the following brief stage directions:

> He is in his early fifties with a hard weathered face and gray forlorn eyes. He wears a sweat-stained gray hat and a cheap dark blue suit. His shoes are brown and brand new.

Doc Golightly's costume introduces him simply and economically as a poor man on a rare visit to the big city. The new shoes tell us that this trip to New York is a big deal for Doc, who tends to be countrified, shabby and 'weathered'. The contrast between his old blue suit and his new brown shoes gives us the keynote to his fish-out-of-water demeanour.

Costume can also convey aspects of backstory. Consider, for example, Miss Havisham in *Great Expectations*. Here is a woman who continues to wear the faded, tattered wedding dress in which she was jilted, decades before. The dress symbolises Miss Havisham's refusal to resolve her tragic past. It is a visual reminder of how she dwells constantly on the pain of her youth.

Or consider the equally tragic Blanche Dubois in Tennessee Williams' classic, *Streetcar Named Desire*. Despite her new, humble surroundings, Blanche continues to wear the moth-eaten feathers and furs of her younger days as a Southern Belle. Using this visual code allows the writer to flag subtle information about her history and motivation to the audience. Such small details can be complemented or compounded in action or dialogue. Her rough-hewn brother-in-law, Stanley, ridicules her clothes and degrades her as a pretentious, out-of-date wanna-be.

In the classic 1940s' script for *All About Eve*, writer Joseph Man-kiewicz gives us a fairly anonymous physical sketch before evoking the image of protagonist Margo Channing as contradictory, strong-willed and slightly desperate.

CLOSE-UP—Margo Channing

She sits at Max's left, at DeWitt's right. An attractive, strong face. She is childish, adult, reasonable, unreasonable—usually one when she should be the other, but always positive. She pours a stiff drink.

Note that this portrait is strengthened by a clear gesture and action.

Dialogue

Good screenwriting is governed by a less-is-more aesthetic, where every word and idea is carefully chosen for the contribution it makes to the whole. As we have seen, this works for both stage directions and for dialogue.

There are two aspects of dialogue to consider when writing a screenplay:

- *content* of information to be conveyed to move the plot forward
- *style* of individual character portrayal.

Dialogue should be pithy and sparing. It should serve the larger needs of the following important structures:

- the protagonist's arc
- the plot or main storyline
- the individual scene.

Most importantly, the writer should remember their premise when creating dialogue. If in doubt about what a character would say or do next, consider your premise or guiding concept. Ask yourself: What am I trying to prove here? How can I use this character to demonstrate my central idea or purpose to the audience?

Strong dialogue style

How can you create good dialogue? When putting words in the characters' mouths, the writer must balance two stylistic tendencies: one idealised and one colloquial or everyday.

In 'real life', we tend to wander in our speech and get lost in circles or unfinished lines. In comparison to 'real' speech, screen dialogue is generally idealised speech. Screen dialogue makes a lot more sense than real speech and is usually grammatically more correct than our 'real everyday' speech, which is full of 'ums, ers' and inconsistencies. Screen dialogue conveys many more complete and pointed ideas than does real speech. Unlike real people in the real world, screen characters tend to deliver complex and complete concepts in short one-liners.

Dialogue can reveal many aspects of your characters' backstory. For instance, your choice of words and expression will convey important details about a character's class, race, history and motives.

Consider how your characters' speech patterns and quirks can convey very specific information about their background and attitudes to the audience. Use your dialogue to reveal your characters' backstories. For instance, you might use slang or colloquial expressions to add spice and help to locate your story in a particular historical or class milieu. A character who refers to police as 'screws' has probably had a background in prison, while one who refers to them as 'pigs' may be using the period slang of the 1960s.

Observe dialogue in your favourite screenplays and you may conclude that good lines are inevitably idealised; they are brief and tend to be far neater and more direct than the speech of real life.

They must also be appropriate for the moment. Look at action heroes like Dirty Harry ('make my day!') or the android in Terminator ('I'll be back.') These characters don't say much. Their writers obey the 'less-is-more' aesthetic. Their lines are famous however due to their sharp, poetic intent and their total appropriateness to the action which gives them full meaning.

It's a paradox that good dialogue should also reflect the fragmented and informal nature of spoken language. Writers must study closely the difference between idealised and colloquial dialogue before they will be able to create convincing characters. It takes practice to know the difference between 'stilted' dialogue that is simply too 'word perfect' and 'naturalistic' dialogue that maintains some natural human quirks but remains true to the overall aim: to provide information that reveals character and drives the plot.

Here are some easy guidelines:

- Remember that your dialogue is used in the service of character and needs to convey subtle hints about class, location, ethnicity, and so on.
- Avoid hackneyed phrasing, clichés and lines that feel predictable. These 'clunkers' are easier to detect on screen than they are on the page and reduce the quality of the dialogue.
- To check your dialogue, *read your lines out loud with a friend.* That way, the cadences and patterns of speech can be checked in 'real time'. Dialogue is often glossed over during silent reading. The best test may be a reading done with live actors who can expose the flavour, the authenticity and the potential interpretations of the lines.

Maintain the flow of dialogue

Once the initial stage directions introduce or establish a scene, try not to interrupt the flow of your dialogue with more stage directions unless it is to indicate that something very dramatic happens mid-scene. For instance, if we need to know that one character suddenly grabs another and kisses them (or hits them), include this action when it actually happens.

It is not usual to bracket adverbs such as 'angrily' or 'sadly' into bits of dialogue. If the writer is paying proper attention to the order and content of scenes, they won't need to instruct the actor on how to deliver a line. Writers shouldn't overload the dialogue with such interruptions. Rather, take more care to build emotion where it should really be—in the context of the action and dialogue. If a character is really angry, we should know this by the entire situation, by the action and by the tone of the scene. Inserting the word 'angrily' into a stage direction won't save a scene that lacks all other appropriate indicators of 'anger' in mood or tone.

After completing all the exercises outlined in chapters 1–7 you may now be ready to move forward and to complete the seven-step outline, the plot breakdown, the scene breakdown and the first draft of your screenplay. Remember to discuss your characters and issues with others who may help you articulate ideas. Try to stick to the framework of the four Ps, to manage the long haul of the three acts.

Exercise 8

Dialogue

Developing an ear and an eye for dialogue

8.1 The exercise for this chapter involves the use of unusual information-gathering techniques* to assist in your understanding of dialogue.

Take a small tape-recorder and record a minute or two of 'real-life' speech on tape. Transcribe this dialogue directly and exactly on to paper, word-for-word, with no editing process.

Now rewrite and edit the same 'real-life' speech so that it resembles screen dialogue. This means that you will need to 'clean up' the speech by cutting out unclear sounds or completing unfinished sentences.

Notice how many times you need to cut 'um' and 'er' from the speech. Note also how often people trail off in the middle of a sentence without actually completing their idea. It is very clear that we humans often don't make much sense if you take our words out of context. Without being able to see a person, or without having the benefit of the history of the conversation, it is easy to lose track of their speech.

You may now intervene in this text and add sentences or ideas, or even characters, thus giving the scene a direction or purpose or conclusion which the 'real-life' speech may lack. As a result, you may create a brief vignette or self-contained scene out of your fragment of 'reality'.

8.2 Write a paragraph on what we can learn about writing good dialogue as a result of this exercise.

* You may need to do this exercise at home or with someone you know, since recording people's speech can be an infringement of their privacy.

9

Plotlines, subplots and secondary characters

Chapter objective

To identify A-, B-
and C-storylines,
identifying their
function and
interweaving all
plotlines and
secondary
characters.

I n this chapter, we identify the function of
all plotlines and secondary characters and
discuss the protagonist's journey as outlined
by Christopher Vogler in his book *The Writer's
Journey*.

Complex plot structure

Writer/directors such as Robert Altman (*Short Cuts, Nashville*), Tom
Tywker (*Run Lola Run*) and Quentin Tarantino (*Pulp Fiction*) use
a passing parade of diverse, colourful characters to prove a certain
premise. It's not easy to identify a singular, clear-cut protagonist
in *Pulp Fiction* or in many of Altman's works. In *Short Cuts*, the
premise has to do with the ultimately corrupt nature of the

contemporary Los Angeles lifestyle. In *Pulp Fiction*, it has to do with the relentlessly ordinary nature of criminal lowlife. The premise of *Run Lola Run* suggests that life is a gamble and destiny isn't fixed: we each spin the wheel of fate and take our chances.

In *Run Lola Run*, Lola's world is occupied by a set number of support characters who reappear in each of the three retellings of her story. Writer/director Tom Tykwer uses these characters to represent different subplots in his radically circular three-act structure. For instance, there are incidental characters who reappear in each act—the woman with the pram, the man on the bike, the woman in the bank, the friend of Lola's father, the security guard, and so on. In each of the three acts, which are three different versions of the same drama, these characters are cast in a slightly different light, with a slightly different function. In act one, the protagonist runs into the woman with the pram, whom Lola 'sees' or imagines as an abusive harpie. In act three, she runs past the same woman without touching her and this time 'sees' her as a religious evangelist.

In each case, various interpretations or images are projected on to incidental and support characters by the main protagonist as she continues on her run. Lola has different views of the same characters, depending on her journey. They each represent different aspects of herself and bring out different kinds of responses in her. This complex and radical rendering of the support players illustrates aspects of Tykwer's premise: that a protagonist can change their world and succeed against the odds, depending on how alert they are to the possibilities. Luck is what you make of it.

Such 'postmodern' screenplays as *Pulp Fiction* and *Run Lola Run* rely on a strong ensemble of characters who each stand for the writer's guiding concept or idea. But only certain genres—such as the comedy caper or the satire—can best sustain this web-like structure of many story strands.

It takes much skill to manage and organise a multi-strand plot. Too many characters may remove the focus from the protagonist, and the writer may get tied up in knots trying to resolve too many individual subplot issues.

In her book *Scriptwriting Updated*, Linda Aronson explores several advanced and complex templates for the multi-strand plot. (Aronson 2000). Those screenwriters approaching the craft for the first time, however, are encouraged here to limit their story structure to clear and well organised A- and B-plotlines.

Usually a central figure is required to bind the story and make it appealing to the audience. Remember that the most ancient dramatic formulas concern the audience's need to identify with a single individual whose trials reflect their own. A new writer can hone their technique by avoiding stories that highlight too many characters. Some genres, mainly comedy or the buddy/road movie, can incorporate multiple or dual protagonists. In drama, however, the lack of a central protagonist and an excess of support characters and subplots can diffuse or split the audience's focus, resulting in distraction from the main conflict.

Rather than subscribe to the classic linear protagonist's arc, such screenplays emphasise a kind of karmic world view where the interconnectedness of the characters is primary.

For our purposes, it is advisable to keep the number of subplots and key support roles to a minimum. Too much complexity can prevent a clear through-line from emerging. Let genre be your guide. Isolate and examine the key subplots of your favourite screenplays and observe how they work. A detailed sketch of your story's central plotlines will be an essential working tool and is part of the exercise at the end of this chapter.

Subplots

In chapter 3, we discussed how you can build psychological conflict out of the tension and clashes between the protagonist's different realms—the realm of work and romance; the realm of the battlefield and home; the realm of the spaceship and the home planet, and so on. These realms are often dictated by the genre. They are always associated with one or other of the main support characters—such as the love interest or the antagonist—who act to complicate the protagonist's dramatic problem.

It helps the writer to consider these realms when organising various subplots—the narrative strands that are selected and woven together to form the main story and its complications.

The classic story is organised around a central storyline or plotline, which is technically known as the A-line or A-plot. Parts of the plot which deviate from the main through-line of this central story are known as 'subplots'. There are usually one or more subplots, which may be called the B- and C-lines. These subsidiary parts of the story are interwoven through and around the main storyline or A-plot. They usually correspond with the protagonist's key support roles—the antagonist, the love interest, the buddy, and so on. Subplots add dimension to your script and give it depth.

The main storyline, or A-line, usually focuses on a key arena or realm of the protagonist's life, such as their work or career. The other subplots will represent other realms—the world of romance, the haunted house, the battleground, the criminal underworld, the space ship, or whatever the genre dictates.

Your selection of support characters will be influenced by the genre. For instance, the film *noir* may require a certain kind of detective hero (hardboiled) and a certain kind of love interest (femme fatale). A science fiction film may require a certain kind of spaceship captain and a certain kind of alien leader; a horror film will require a certain kind of monster and a certain kind of victim, and so on. It is up to each writer to understand the 'classic' versions of generic stories and characters and then to make creative decisions about how closely they stick to the classic form and how far they depart from the norm.

To organise your plot structure, you may relate your two main A- and B-plotlines to different realms of the protagonist's life and to different characters within those realms. Let's use a metaphor from live theatre to understand the use of subplots. When the writer develops a subplot, it's as if they take the audience aside from the main storyline. Each subplot allows us to glimpse a realm that is adjacent to the main stage or arena of action.

In theory, each of the subplots, and the support characters that go with them, has its own goal, obstacles and climax. The writer needs to interweave these subplots so that they intersect or come together at the main turning points. This means that the protagonist will often confront key support players in a situation of conflict at various turning points throughout the story.

The writer will usually resolve the tension and conflict between different characters in the climax, or grand finale.

Interweaving plotlines A and B

Your protagonist may have two conflicting goals which are associated with two plotlines. For example, you may be writing an urban comedy about a city girl who is strung-out between her love life and her career. In this case, think of the world of her romance as the A-line of the story and the world of her career as the B-line.

Each plotline has its own goal. For instance, the protagonist may want to spend time with her love interest, but on the other hand, she may also want a job promotion. It's easy for the writer to twist these two plotlines into a problem for the protagonist, so that the different goals of her A- and B-plotlines are in conflict.

For instance, the inciting incident may establish how the protagonist is under pressure from her boyfriend to go away for a romantic weekend. We can call this plotline A, which belongs to the realm of romance. The writer may then create conflict between the A-line (romance) and the B-line (realm of work) by putting the protagonist under more pressure from her boss. What if she is ordered to finish an important office report on the same weekend that her boyfriend wants to see her?

The writer may then provide a deadline for both plotlines. The boyfriend may threaten to leave her if she doesn't commit to the romantic weekend. The boss may threaten to dismiss or 'fire' her if she doesn't complete the report on the same weekend. This conflicting deadline adds up to a convincing dramatic problem or dilemma for the protagonist: she cannot achieve her work goal without losing her lover and vice versa. Either way, she seems set to lose something, no matter what she does.

Subplots can be used to help focus problems for your characters. Chronology is central to all this. The above example features a deadline (the weekend) to underscore the tension between the subplots. The story is partly structured by our knowledge that the protagonist has until the weekend to sort out her problem in both arenas—in plotline A and plotline B.

The timeline for one subplot may close off some time before that of the main action. For instance, in our urban comedy, the heroine may decide to drop her boyfriend if she finds out that he is jealous of her work. This may represent a termination of the A-line. Or it may represent a temporary closure of this plotline, as there is a chance that the romance may be picked up again later in the action.

Whenever the writer resolves one plotline, this often triggers the resolution of the other plotline. If the ending is to be well-resolved and exciting, the writer needs to entwine the two plotlines quite closely together.

One very common pattern is that the climax of the story (the act three turning point) brings together both subplots in a grand finale. In such a case, the heroine may be finalising the important report for her boss when her boyfriend shows up unexpectedly in her office with two airline tickets to a tropical island. In this scenario, the protagonist has to act *now*, decisively, to solve her dilemma. When this deadline arrives, the two competing subplots come together at the same time. At this point of climax, the audience must ask 'How can she solve this problem? What will happen next?'

Will she take the airline tickets and run with her boyfriend? Or will she stay in the office and finish her report? The writer must orchestrate tensions between the A and B plotlines to create an exciting sense of conflict and suspense as the protagonist finds her way out of or into 'double trouble'.

While the style or subject matter of this urban comedy may not apply to audiences who live outside of big cities, the structure of the protagonist's problem has universal relevance. This kind of classic dilemma, or 'double bind', is the stuff of great comedy and drama. Why? Because it reflects the structure of problems that are familiar to most human beings. We all have competing interests in our lives. This typical human problem is represented by two

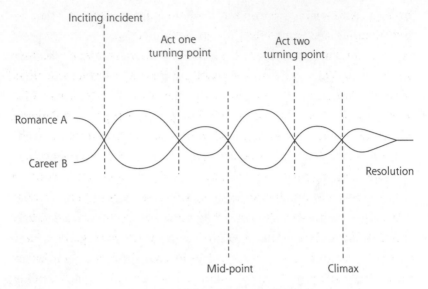

Inciting incident

Act one
turning point

Act two
turning point

Romance A

Career B

Resolution

Mid-point

Climax

Figure 9.1   Interweaving A and B plotlines

plotlines that each put pressure on the protagonist. Figure 7.1 shows how the A-plotline and B-plotline may merge together, creating conflict for the protagonist at major turning points.

Secondary characters

Linda Seger suggests that one of the writer's key questions is 'Who is necessary, besides my protagonist, for telling this story? Who does my major character need around him or her?'

By answering these questions, Seger suggests, 'you will prevent yourself from arbitrarily adding characters to the story, and will begin to understand . . . the balance between the main characters and the supporting characters, and not to confuse the story by overloading it with people'. (Seger 1990, p. 121).

A secondary or support role, such as the antagonist or the love interest, provides a glimpse of exotic worlds apart from the main action, adding colour and contrast to the world of the protagonist. However, don't be tempted to include support roles and subplots just for added colour. Remember that their function is to illuminate the action and motivation of the main character and the main storyline.

Syd Field discusses the function of the support characters in relation to the main character. He cautions the writer to remember that support roles don't actually have a 'life' of their own. Their main function is to tell us something about the protagonist. Field refers to the great novelist Henry James and his 'theory of illumination'. He suggests that we consider the protagonist as standing in the centre of a circle, surrounded by all the support roles, whose only function is to illuminate the main character. (Field 1984, p. 71).

Imagine your protagonist standing at the centre of a dark stage. The support roles shouldn't distract us from the action at centre-stage. Each support player has their own degree of colour and life, but their main function is to hold a torch, the light from which is aimed at the protagonist. While support roles may allow us a glimpse into another story realm, their main function is to show the audience a different aspect of the central character. This ensures that the emotional and dramatic focus is riveted on the protagonist, who is the main figure for audience identification.

Characters and point-of-view

Support characters help to indicate the protagonist's point of view. In providing a sounding board or a catalyst for the protagonist,

177

they tell us something concrete about the main character and their attitudes, and help to highlight the tensions in their world. They also help to move the plot forward by indicating how the protagonist is progressing through their journey. Various support roles also provide different angles on the action. They allow the audience a different point-of-view or vantage point from which to assess the unfolding drama.

Support players may also tell us something further about the writer's themes and premise. Indirectly, they indicate something about the writer's attitude by expressing and representing diverse voices and ideas.

Four questions are helpful for a writer who is trying to identify the nature of their secondary or support characters:

- What aspect of human nature does the character represent?
- What does this character need from the protagonist and vice versa?
- What does this character tell us about the protagonist?
- How does this character move the story forward?

While interacting with support characters such as the love interest or the antagonist, the protagonist reveals changes in their motivation and actions. This means that the writer can use subplots or realms associated with secondary roles to illustrate changes in the self-perception, emotional growth and motivation of the protagonist. These changes express the writer's viewpoint on human life and emotions.

For instance, in a complex structure typical of the drama genre, the A-line may follow the story of a protagonist, a cop or a lawyer, as he deals with a criminal. This antagonist represents the opposite of the protagonist—the dark side of crime, violence, greed and corruption. Scenes of contrast between the protagonist and the antagonist can therefore highlight what the protagonist stands for—decency, law and order.

In more recent versions of the classic good guy/bad guy conflict, writers may put a unique 'spin' on the formula. For instance, there may be a mysterious attraction between the protagonist and the antagonist. In *Basic Instinct*, this classic structure of opposites, between the protagonist and the antagonist, is subverted. Here, the 'bad guys' are all played by women, who function as a mixture of the familiar femme fatale role and the antagonist role.

The protagonist, Detective Nick Curran, actually falls in love with the antagonist, his main suspect, Catherine Trammel. Rather than prove him to be a 'good guy' cop, his interaction with the support characters shows him as an ambiguous character, one who is drawn to the dark side of life—a man who shares character traits with the antagonist he is out to capture. This dynamic between the protagonist and the antagonist reveals or reflects both his heroic aspects and his 'dark side' to the audience.

Character archetypes and anthropology

We have seen how the writer can use support characters and subplots to shape the main plot and move it forward. But what are the deep layers of myth and psychology that affect the way an audience reads the plot?

In *The Savage Mind*, the brilliant French anthopologist Claude Levi-Strauss points to our basic human need to invest meaning in the world around us, using myth and ritual as a way of ordering our surroundings. Within this framework, it is apparent that story-telling is a kind of coping strategy that we humans employ to understand and manage the essential chaos of existence. Myths help us to answer the big universal questions about life: Where did we come from? Who made us? What are we doing here? Why?

In *Man and his Symbols*, the psychologist Carl Jung examines dream states and myth. Jung's great insight is that archetypal characters and images reflect different aspects of human psychology. These archetypes come from an invisible source that springs from deep within us all. Jung called this the 'collective unconscious' of the human race.

In his seminal text, *The Hero with a Thousand Faces*, Joseph Campbell examines the myth cycles of 'the hero', a character type that appears consistently over the centuries on different continents and in different epochs. Campbell points out that these well-worn legends and character types have been reappearing in plays, games, legends and theatrical works consistently throughout history.

Archetypal characters personify human qualities in common figures such as the mother, the innocent, the warrior, the monster, the whore, the patriarch, the villain, the lovers, and so on. Over thousands of years, these characters and their stories have reflected different aspects of humanity. These characters are repeated in the world of myth—the world of our dreams and fantasies. That's why stories based around mythic archetypes have the ring of psychological truth. They are accurate models of the human mind—true maps of the psyche—even when they portray fantastic, impossible or unreal events. Storytellers use their characters to express profound and complex ideas about who we are.

Each of these approaches to storytelling as myth and ritual can tell us much about writing for film. It seems that whichever 'tribe' we belong to humans may only actually know a handful of basic template stories which we keep retelling with endless variations.

These include myths and ancient legends such as *Oedipus* (family tragedy), *Romeo and Juliet* (romance) and *Dracula* (horror).

In *The Writer's Journey*, Christopher Vogler refers to both Jung and Campbell to describe the classic character archetypes which are most useful to the writer. According to Vogler, the most powerful stories feature these familiar myths and characters, '[T]hey are a great key to life as well as a major instrument for dealing more effectively with a mass audience.' (Vogler 1999, p. 11).

Vogler points out that the constantly repeating characters which emerge in dreams, myths, stories and film represent key archetypes that reflect different aspects of the human mind. According to Vogler, stories based on the Hero myth are instantly appealing because they deal with universal themes and characters that reflect humanity in all its variation. (Vogler 1999, p. 36).

In the light of this, Vogler focuses on the journey of the hero as it appears in stories and myths that are as old as language itself. He breaks down the hero's journey into a twelve-stage paradigm. In this scheme, the hero figure is defined as the central protagonist who goes on a journey where he encounters common archetypes that are found in all stories. For the storyteller, these character archetypes are indispensable tools of the trade. You can't tell stories without them.

Chris Vogler's Twelve Steps

Vogler raises two questions which are helpful for a writer trying to identify the nature of an archetype:

- What psychological function or part of the personality does this type represent?
- What is its dramatic function?

Vogler also identifies various stages of the hero's journey that may help writers to structure the journey of the protagonist. As in the model we outlined in the last chapter, there are several key points in the drama which will keep the protagonist moving forward and 'on their toes'. The ups and downs of the journey will also keep the audience hooked into the story. (Vogler 1999, p. 33).

1 The ordinary world

Vogler suggests that most stories are founded on a 'fish out of water idea' which takes the hero out of his ordinary world. The writer's first task is to establish that world before presenting the hero with a problem. (Vogler 1999, p. 15).

2 The call to adventure

This represents the second story stage, where the hero is presented with a problem, challenge or adventure to undertake. This means the hero can no longer remain in the comfort of the Ordinary World. According to Vogler, the Call to Adventure establishes the stakes of the quest—the goals and the challenge.

3 The refusal of the call

This describes how the somewhat reluctant hero feels threatened and afraid as they stand on the threshold of adventure. The hero has not yet committed to the journey. Some other influence—a change in circumstance, or the encouragement of a mentor—is required to get them past this turning point of fear.

4 Mentor

The fourth stage features the hero's mentor, which represents the bond between parent and child, teacher and student, doctor and patient. The mentor may appear in many guises and usually provides the hero with advice, equipment or guidance to push them forward on their journey.

5 Crossing the first threshold

This occurs as the hero agrees to move forward and accept the challenge or the call to adventure. 'The hero, having overcome fear, has decided to confront the problem and take action. She is now committed to the journey and there is no turning back.' (Vogler 1999, p. 18). (This first threshold corresponds to the turning point between acts one and two.)

6 Tests, allies and enemies

Once the hero has crossed the first threshold, they encounter new challenges and tests, make allies and enemies, and begin to learn the rules of the special world. In this special, new environment, the hero obtains information about their quest and learns the new rules that apply to the special world. Vogler points out that several aspects of the hero's character are usually revealed in such scenes. Often, the hero must pass tests while dealing with new characters and encounters along the way.

7 Approach to the Inmost Cave

The hero comes to the 'edge of a dangerous place . . . where the object of the quest is hidden'. (Vogler 1999, p. 20). Vogler suggests that this is often located in the headquarters or lair of the hero's greatest enemy, the most dangerous spot in the special world—the Inmost Cave. At this point, the hero must cross the second major threshold and may pause in order to prepare, plan and outwit the villain's guards. This is the phase of approach, where the hero must confront death or supreme danger.

8   The supreme ordeal

At this point, the fortunes of the hero hit their lowest point. The audience are held in suspense, not knowing if the hero will live or die. The hero is now in a situation of severe misfortune, as they must confront their greatest fears while being on the brink of battle with a hostile force.

Vogler points out that in a lighthearted genre, such as a romantic comedy, the lowest point faced by the hero may simply be the temporary death of the romance. He gives the example of the classic second movement of the standard plot, 'Boy meets girl, boy loses girl, boy gets girl'. Whatever the genre, the hero's chances of getting their prize look bleakest at this point.

Vogler emphasises that this ordeal is a critical moment in any story, as it represents the magic moment when the hero appears to 'die', only to be reborn. The audience is revived by the hero's return from death, giving a feeling of elation and exhilaration. Vogler suggests, '[T]he hero of every story is an initiate being introduced to the mysteries of life and death. Every story needs such a life-or-death moment in which the hero or his goals are in mortal jeopardy.' (Vogler 1999, p. 22). This corresponds to the mid-point.

9   Reward (seizing the sword)

The hero has survived death, beaten the dragon and given the audience cause to celebrate. They now take possession of the treasure they have been seeking—their reward. Vogler points out that 'the sword' is sometimes knowledge and experience that leads to a greater understanding and reconciliation with hostile forces. At this point, the hero may enter into conflict with a character or be reconciled with the love interest. There is often a love scene at this point to celebrate the victory.

> From the hero's point of view, members of the opposite sex may appear to be Shapeshifters, an archetype of change. They seem to shift . . . in form or age, reflecting the confusing and constantly changing aspects of the opposite sex . . . the hero's Supreme Ordeal may grant a better understanding of the opposite sex, an ability to see beyond the shifting outer appearance, leading to a reconciliation. The hero may also become more attractive as a result of having survived the Supreme Ordeal. He has earned the title of 'hero' by having taken the supreme risk on behalf of the community.' (Vogler 1999, p. 23).

10   The road back

This point takes the hero into the third and final act as they deal with the consequences of confronting the dark forces of the supreme ordeal. If they remain unreconciled with their partner, the gods or the hostile forces, they may come raging after them. Vogler points out that 'chase scenes often spring up at this point, as the hero is pursued on The Road Back by the vengeful forces she has disturbed by Seizing the sword, the elixir or the treasure'. (Vogler 1999, p. 24).

This stage marks the hero's decision to return to the ordinary world. The special world must be left behind, but there are still dangers, temptations and tests ahead.

11   Resurrection

Vogler refers to the way ancient hunters and warriors had to be cleansed after battle before they returned to their communities. The hero who has been in the realm of the dead must be reborn and purified in one last deathly ordeal and resurrection before returning to the Ordinary World of the living. He suggests that this moment is almost a replay of The Supreme Ordeal, as death and darkness reappear before finally being defeated. It is the final test for the hero, who must be tested once more to see if they have really learned the lessons of the supreme ordeal. 'The hero is transformed by these moments of death and rebirth and returns to ordinary life reborn with new insights.' (Vogler 1999, p. 24).

12   Return with the elixir

The hero returns at the end of act three to the Ordinary World with some Elixir (magical healing potion), treasure or lesson from the Special World. 'Sometimes the Elixir is treasure won on the quest, but it may be love, freedom, wisdom, or the knowledge that the Special World exists and can be survived.' (Vogler 1999, p. 25). Vogler points out that, in many comedies, the foolish hero may be doomed to repeat the adventure as they refuse to learn their lesson and embark on the same folly that got them into trouble in the first place. Vogler's paradigm provides a useful reference for the construction of your protagonist's journey. It emphasises the need for a dynamic protagonist and solid support roles within a complex moral universe.

EXERCISE 9

Biographies for key support roles

9.1 Having reviewed your premise and your main plot and protagonist, now identify the protagonist's support characters and their storylines.

a. Look at the genre you are working in and figure out what types of characters are essential to your story.

b. Rework the character biographies for your support characters. Remember that we are interested in their history mainly as it relates to the protagonist. Consider their aims, goals, needs and wants in relation to the main character. Tell us about the realms they operate in. What does all this tell us about your protagonist?

c. How do your two main support characters illuminate the protagonist's problem and psychology?

d. Briefly outline the journey of your support characters using the seven-step outline from chapter 10.

9.2 Look at the rules of your genre and use the following questions to help plan your subplots:

a. What function does each of your secondary characters serve in re-inforcing the protagonist's journey?

b. How will you set up the support characters in relation to the protagonist?

c. Is the realm or world of the support characters shown or implied?

d. What strengths and weaknesses does each secondary character possess?

e. Does your story need an antagonist and/or love interest?

f. How believable is your antagonist?

g. How does the key support role illuminate the protagonist?

h. How does the key support role create a sharp contrast for your protagonist?

i. What are the objectives of the secondary characters? (Remember: even though the function of the secondary characters is to help in the unfolding of the protagonist's journey, they have their own needs, goals, strengths and weaknesses.)

j. How do you propose to resolve the secondary characters' conflicts?

10

Act one structure

Chapter objective
To shape the
structure of act one,
based on the seven-
step outline.

I n the last chapter, we saw how a writer can
invest their work with mythical resonance
using character archetypes. We also saw how your three acts can
be broken down according to a framework consisting of the main
storyline, or plotline A, and subplots known as the B-line and the
C-line. These plotlines correspond to different realms in the
protagonist's world and to different characters within these realms.

In chapter 6, we introduced a useful outline based on the
classic three-act structure. We will now develop a seven-step
outline which lists the key turning points of your story.

The seven-step outline should account for every crucial structural support in your plot. It begins with a set-up line in which
you must commit to a clear vision of your protagonist and of the
world or realm in which we first meet them.

The final step in your seven-step outline describes the story's
resolution—the moments after the climax, when the writer

189

suggests how the protagonist actually responds to the climax and how they aim towards the future.

In the chapter 6 exercise, you began developing a seven-step outline by focusing on seven plot points. In the chapter 9 exercise, you outlined the journeys of your secondary characters. Now we can incorporate these plot points and the research found in your folio into a seven-step outline that focuses on your protagonist's journey over three acts. To achieve this, you may consider how to select the key moments in your protagonist's story that represent the most crucial point of change or drama in their 'life' at this time.

The seven-step outline: The road-map of your protagonist's journey

Each step in your outline may only be one sentence long. It can be a complex sentence with more than one clause, but it must follow on logically from the previous sentence. This ensures that your story builds on what you establish as the foundation and follows in a logical cause-and-effect order.

1. set-up of the protagonist and their world
2. inciting incident
3. act one turning point
4. mid-point
5. act two turning point
6. act three turning point (climax)
7. resolution or denouement.

Here is an important tip: when writing your outline, begin each line with your protagonist's name. This puts them always at the centre of the action and ensures that you stick to the main story-line, which is your proper focus.

Step 1: The set-up

Establish the protagonist and their world with a brief sketch of where they are and what they do, their central need, goal and/or problem. (You only have a few words to do this, which means your choice of words will be the result of careful thought.)

Step 2: The inciting incident

Describe how the protagonist you set up in step 1 responds when they are challenged by an event that shifts the course of the action and affects their goal or need by presenting a central dramatic problem and conflict.

Step 3: Act one turning point

Describe the protagonist's response to a further shift or complication that adds more conflict and heat to their main problem.

Step 4: Mid-point

Describe the protagonist's response as they hit their lowest ebb when the central problem threatens to overcome them.

Step 5: Act two turning point

Describe the protagonist's response to a key conflict that is the result of their central problem. Consider how this must steer the drama towards the climax of act three.

Step 6: The climax—act three turning point

Describe the protagonist's response when all the key elements of the problem come into conflict at once.

Step 7: The resolution

Describe how the protagonist resolves or deals with the outcome of all this—do they ride off into the sunset; do they get the money *and* the girl; do they get the girl, but not the money? Cap the story off and tie up all the key storylines.

Balancing the first and last turning points

Now you are going to take a closer look at the first and last turning points of your story outline. What makes these two points so important? Considering the first and last moments of your story will help you to realise and grasp your story as a whole, entire entity.

The clues about character and plot which you 'seed', or plant, in the very beginning will be crucial to the ending. These clues help you to set up the appropriate details to be 'paid off' later, in the climax. It is therefore important to understand your climax even *before* you write the beginning. This allows you to understand what you are aiming for when you set up your story in the first act.

The first and last turning points of a script encapsulate the changes undergone by the protagonist as they respond to the dramatic problem. These crucial signposts set the tone and mood of the story for the audience. They frame the entire story, providing the supportive pillars on which the entire structure rests. Review the first and last turning points of your plot outline and identify your protagonist's journey. Do the plot points between the first and last turning points support that journey?

The outlining process will help you to get your four Ps interlocked and in shape. Without a 'map' for these key structures —protagonist, problem, plot and premise—gaps in the plot will inevitably appear. Essentially, the outline helps you to trouble-shoot your screenplay before you begin drafting it. The process requires discipline and a focus on the logic of the story. However, once mastered, this short document will provide you with a concept that is manageable and easy to discuss with others.

The outline also allows you to diagnose and troubleshoot most major plot problems so that there will be fewer surprises during your long first draft. If you have done a good job on a tight outline, the time and effort will have been well spent. This process removes the element of doubt from the writing process. Having outlined the main action, you *know* what your characters will do next and they will do it.

Act one—step 1: The set-up—establish the protagonist and their world

Now that you have begun to think about the story as a whole, it's time to focus on the opening in a very specific way. We have already discussed the importance of seducing the audience with a sympathetic protagonist, one they can identify with and relate to.

Act one commences with the set-up of the world you want to explore. Focus on your premise and use this to help you frame a sense of the protagonist's goals and fears. Choose your adjectives carefully to 'pin down' and prioritise the complex character of your protagonist.

Think carefully about the cinematic potential of your locations. Review chapter 3 and consider how the work you have done on location and story realms can express or externalise your protagonist's psychology.

• Note that the opening scene signals the flavour or tone of the whole story.

• Consider how these scenes illustrate your themes. Remember, you are setting up what needs to be paid off by the end of the story: your premise.

Act one—step 2: The inciting incident

The protagonist's main problem or conflict needs to be introduced, or at least set up, in the first fifteen minutes of screen-time, preferably at around pages 10–15 of the script. This point is the inciting incident or catalyst. It describes a scene or event that introduces the central problem, and forces the protagonist to begin their journey. The inciting incident upsets their world in a way that cannot simply be put right.

• The inciting incident may represent the opening point of a particular subplot—plotline B—the introduction of the love interest or the antagonist. The protagonist may thus glimpse or enter another realm at this point.

• What story device have you chosen to 'hook' the audience and move your story forward? For example, in *Thelma & Louise*, we meet both protagonists in their respective kitchens—one is a disgruntled housewife at home, the other is at work, waiting tables in a restaurant. Both women seem limited by the trivial drudgery of their kitchen routines. The inciting incident occurs after they stop for a drink at a roadside bar—a realm of freedom compared to the environment where we first encounter them. When Louise shoots the attacker in the carpark, the action takes a totally new turn and the women hit the highway. This is to be their realm of action for the rest of the story.

Act one—step 3: The act one turning point

The event that comes at the end of act one often compounds the dramatic problem of the inciting incident and is a point of no return. A turning point must make the protagonist change their direction. This change should, in turn, lead to a new problem or intensify the problem that you established in the inciting incident. For example, the protagonist's relationship with a key support role (love interest, buddy or antagonist) may now lead them away from the realm of the main storyline into the realm of plotline B.

Ask yourself the following questions:

- How does your character respond when they are challenged by an event that shifts the course of the action?
- How does this affect their main goal/need?
- How does it test their attitudes/beliefs?
- How can you use this incident to help express your premise?

Your third step should briefly contain the answers to these questions. Remember, it is not just the event we are interested in, but also the protagonist's *response* to the event. *This response is what defines them*; the event itself is just a trigger or stimulus.

For example, the act one turning point in *Thelma & Louise* occurs when Louise calls her boyfriend Jimmy and asks him to send her some money. This moment affects the main goal or need by confirming the women's decision to remain on the run, rather than go back home. Louise's phone call tests their attitudes by presenting the basic challenge of survival outside the law. It perfectly introduces the story's general premise: that it's better to die free than to live in captivity or prison.

In this first part of the outline, you have established your protagonist and a central dramatic problem. In the next chapter, you will work on act two, devising more plot points, problems and obstacles to complicate the story even further.

While constructing act one, remember to stay focused on your ending. All story elements must be set up to lead the audience towards a strong conclusion. The audience never knows what will happen next in the story. The author, however, must know exactly how each scene leads in a logical chain of cause-and-effect towards a well-planned climax.

EXERCISE 10

Your set-up

By focusing on the major turning points, it is possible to write a concise outline of your story. The seven steps of the outline act as a model for your entire story structure.

Remember that your act one set-up will be reflected in your ending. Considering that you have an idea of your ending, let's review your beginning set-up. Have you chosen the appropriate starting point?

Remember, also, that the opening scene signals the flavour or tone of the whole story. Think of how your protagonist will resolve their problem. What will be the final outcome? Does your protagonist ride off into the sunset; do they get the money *and* the lover; do they get the lover, but not the money?

To prepare for your own outline, revise act one of your favourite screenplays and identify the scenes or events that comprise the set-up, the inciting incident and the first turning point of each.

If you have trouble accessing screenplays, do some research in the genre of your choice and apply the same technique to several films, taking note of their structure and turning points. Note, however, that you will do better to read screenplays rather than watch the finished product on the screen.

Bear this kind of 'big picture' perspective in mind as you shape the structure of your story. Select scenes or events that follow the seven-step outline points listed on pages 190–2.

Act one

Step 1: The set-up

Establish the protagonist and their world with a brief sketch of where they are and what they do, their central need, goal and/or problem.

* Identify four or five scenes or events which, when juxtaposed, reveal the protagonist's world, their strengths and weaknesses, and their needs, fears and desires. Juxtapositions of very different kinds of scenes or events can flag or foreshadow the emotional range and themes that are to be dealt with. Remember, you are setting up what needs to be paid off by the end of the story

Step 2: The inciting incident

Describe how the character you set up in step 1 responds when they are challenged by an event that shifts the course of the action and affects their goal or need by presenting a central dramatic problem and conflict.

* Identify the inciting incident and any scenes that develop it as a problem or conflict.
* Does the inciting incident result from conflicts between different characters/different realms/different goals and values in the protagonist's inner and outer worlds? How do these add up to a specific problem or dilemma?
* Does the inciting incident represent the opening point of a particular subplot—plotline B—the introduction of the love interest or the antagonist? The protagonist may enter another realm at this point.

Step 3: Act one turning point

Describe the protagonist's response to a further shift or complication that adds more conflict and heat to their main problem. The turning point must make the protagonist change their direction. This change should, in turn, lead to a new problem or intensify the key problem that you established in the inciting incident.

- Shape three or four scenes that build up to the turning point and reveal your protagonist's reactions.
- How does this course of events change the protagonist and the direction of the story?
- How does this affect their main goal/need?
- How does it test their attitudes/beliefs?
- How does it change their world?

11

Act two structure

Chapter objective

To shape the structure of act two, based on the seven-step outline.

Your seven-step outline is a road-map for your protagonist's journey. We have seen how act one contains the first three steps of your outline: the set-up, the inciting incident and the act one turning point. The set-up (step 1) consists of several scenes which establish the protagonist and their world. The inciting incident (step 2) is the event that creates a central problem. The act one turning point (step 3) is a sequence that complicates the central problem—ensuring that the protagonist's life will never be the same and catapulting them in to an emotional journey.

In this chapter, we examine act two: the battleground where the protagonist and the premise are tested.

Act two: The long march forward

It's easy writing the first act of a screenplay. Why? From the writer's viewpoint, act one usually unfolds in a rush. You have fun creating a likeable protagonist and devising a juicy problem or dilemma to put them in. Your imaginary audience is eagerly soaking up the clues you are providing for them about the protagonist and their world. They are busy learning 'the rules' of the universe that you have created for their amusement.

In the last chapter, you provided an outline for act one that will 'hook' your audience. Now comes the real challenge—act two. Traditionally, new writers seem to 'blow' all their energy in the first act and then 'run out of steam' in act two. How can you avoid writer's burnout and keep your audience tuned-in?

Think of your screenplay as a continent to be explored. The difficult middle stretch is like a great desert that lies at the heart of your story. The road is long and the terrain so dry that the story may actually die before it's finished. Your job is to bypass the desert and provide a fascinating landscape for the audience. If you cannot sustain the interest you established in the first 25 to 30 minutes of act one, you might as well kiss your story goodbye.

Remember that you are constructing drama, and that means creating conflict. So, another way to look at act two is to see it as an emotional battlefield through which the protagonist must manoeuvre in order to survive. Put your protagonist in jeopardy— that is, put them in a high-risk situation where they could lose something or be badly harmed *if* they cannot solve their dramatic problem. This will make the audience care about the outcome. Refer to your premise to remind yourself of what your focus should be.

Your major concern is the structuring of dramatic conflict. And dramatic conflict begins with character psychology and the manipulation of time to create tension in the plot.

- Remind yourself of what your protagonist wants/desires, needs and fears.
- Create several obstacles that will challenge your protagonist in their attempt to meet their goals.

In act two, you add more conflicting twists and unexpected turns in the form of barriers and complications in order to catch the protagonist (and the audience) off guard. Rather than fall asleep, the audience must be asking, 'What will happen next?' Give them plenty to worry about. Let's examine ways of doing this by focusing on step four of your seven-step outline.

Act two—step 4: The mid-point

One rule of thumb is that by the middle of act two—also known as the mid-point—your main character should be in a pit of grim despair. They have reached the lowest point in their character arc, the lowest ebb of their life force. It's your job to get them there.

How can you extract the most audience empathy for this character? Think of your protagonist's fears and foibles. Then think of the *worst possible thing* that could happen to this person, and then make it happen.

In *The Writer's Journey*, Christopher Vogler studies heroic myth and the screenplay form. He suggests that act two contains the crisis that separates the two main parts of your story. In Vogler's scheme, the protagonist's main crisis or ordeal may come at the mid-point *or* at the end of act two, at the turning point. This contrasts with the traditional three-act paradigm, where the low point is situated at the mid-point.

According to Vogler, there are two potential locations for dramatic crisis: the central crisis and the delayed crisis.

> The **central crisis** has the advantage of symmetry and leaves plenty of time for elaborate consequences to flow from the ordeal . . . it allows for another critical moment or turning point at the end of Act Two. (Vogler 1999, p. 161).

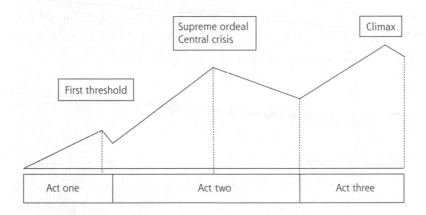

Major dramatic high points in a story with a central crisis

(Courtesy of Chris Vogler, *The Writer's Journey*)

Figure 11.1   Three-act structure: The central crisis

Vogler suggests that the writer may also delay the main crisis until the *end* of act two. Using this technique, the pace of the second act is considerably slower, as the writer needs a longer, more gradual build-up to the big moment. Figure 11.2 illustrates the onscreen chronology required to delay the 'central' crisis until the end of act two.

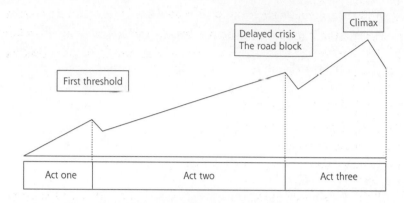

Major dramatic high points in a story with a delayed crisis

(Courtesy of Chris Vogler, *The Writer's Journey*)

Figure 11.2   Three-act structure: The delayed crisis

How to raise the stakes

Whichever option you choose, you need to raise the stakes all through the story so that it seems to build relentlessly towards the climax at the end. The most classic approach is to use the mid-point as the protagonist's lowest ebb and then use the act two turning point (step 5 in your outline) to mark the slow, steady build towards the act three climax.

In act two, the writer must take hold of the dramatic problem that has been established in act one, and complicate, amplify and elaborate on it. Remember to keep your premise in mind at all stages of the outline.

Keep asking yourself the following questions to help structure your decisions about plot:

- What am I trying to prove here?
- What is my central concept?

You can use several structural resources to put more pressure on your protagonist. It's possible to keep producing more twists in the plot by observing the structures that you have explored in previous chapters:

- Look at your backstory.
- Look at your secondary characters.
- Look at your subplots.
- Look at your character biographies.

Look closely at your genre to discover the rules and requirements of your story type. These will help you to figure out what the audience will be expecting at different points along the way. For example, if you are working in the action adventure mode, in act two the hero may be threatened with death if he can't engineer an escape from his dilemma. Engineer an escape and then, when the audience thinks he is free at last, reverse the situation by adding further obstacles and complications that foil him and keep him from achieving his goal.

Barriers, complications and reversals

Let's look at several story devices you can use to put your protagonist in trouble and keep them there, at least for the mid-section of your plot.

In her book *Making a Good Script Great*, Linda Seger suggests that you drive your story forward with 'action points'. Seger defines these as 'actions which demand a response' by the protagonist. She also refers to three main types of action point: the barrier, the complication and the reversal. (Seger 1994, p. 62).

First, consider the way your character can hit a barrier and must change direction or try another action in order to move forward towards success. The barrier forces a character to take a new direction or make a new decision.

Seger has observed in great detail how barriers can be employed by the screenwriter to keep act two moving. She points out that barriers stop the action for a moment. The character goes around the barrier and the action continues. Seger explains, '[T]he story doesn't develop out of the barrier, it develops out of the decision to try another action.' (Seger 1994, p. 63). Barriers lead to further action, but the real development and momentum comes as a result of the last action, when the character overcomes a barrier.

For example, in *Run Lola Run* the heroine must get money to her boyfriend or he will be killed by bad guys. Lola decides to ask her father for help, but he refuses (a barrier). She then decides to rob his bank. In the next act of Lola's story, she arrives at her father's bank to find him missing (a barrier). She then decides to gamble for money at a casino and wins the jackpot (a reversal).

Consider also the complication, which Seger describes as a kind of set-up for a future conflict or obstacle. Something happens, but the protagonist's reaction comes later at the pay-off. The audience has to wait for the complication to come to fruition. They must anticipate the inevitable response or perhaps be surprised by it. According to Seger, a complication doesn't turn the story around; it keeps the story moving forward.

For example, in *Thelma & Louise*, two friends are simply trying to get away for the weekend. They are waylaid by a rapist (a barrier). They shoot him and make a get-away (a response). The two women are stopped again by a hitch-hiker (a complication) who seduces Thelma (a complication) and then robs the women (a complication). The hitch-hiker is then picked up by the police.

These complications are all paid-off when he reveals the women's intended destination, producing a major shift in the drama.

The response of the dual protagonists to these barriers and complications drives the plot in acts two and three. These complications are paid-off along the way and culminate in the conclusion, when Thelma and Louise decide finally to die, rather than go to jail. In this example, the barriers and complications help the writer to prove her premise: it is better to die free than to suffer unjust imprisonment.

Seger correctly observes that the strongest action point is a reversal. This changes the direction of the story 180 degrees. It makes the story move from a positive to a negative direction, or vice versa. It's a complete turnaround that can work physically or emotionally by reversing the action or the emotional direction of a story. One or even two reversals placed as the turning points at the end of act one and/or the mid-point, can be used to great effect to push the story forward through act two. (Seger 1994, p. 66).

An example of a reversal occurs at the end of act one in *Thelma & Louise*. The two protagonists arrive at a roadside bar and celebrate their freedom. Their joy turns to horror, however, when Thelma is nearly raped and Louise defends her, killing the offender. This first major reversal spins the tone of the story from one of carefree road comedy to one of tension and suspense.

Another reversal in *Thelma & Louise* occurs near the end of act two. Both women are enjoying tender moments with their lovers, but their happiness evaporates as they discover that one of the men has stolen all their money. The audience's mood shifts rapidly, following the highs and lows of the dual protagonists as they confront these reversals in order to pursue their journey.

In *Breakfast at Tiffany's*, the would-be lovers, Holly and Paul, fight and break up at the mid-point, thus casting doubt on the protagonist's ability to carry-through with the romance. The writer thus creates a reversal from love to tragedy, as we realise that Holly may lose her lover.

The more the protagonist has to lose, the more the audience will care about the outcomes. This is known as raising the stakes.

Use support roles to provide barriers, obstacles and reversals

If there is an antagonist in your screenplay, use this support character in act two to put more heat or pressure on the protagonist. They will provide barriers to success and set-ups in suspense that will be paid off later.

The love interest can fulfil a similar role. If there is a love interest, create some real conflict in act two so that the lovers are no longer together or must face some serious barrier or reversal in their situation. Raise the stakes again and again so that the audience experiences heightened suspense.

Act two—step five: Act two turning point

You will spend the first part of act two getting your protagonist into what Vogler calls 'the supreme ordeal'—the pit of self-doubt and misery. Spend the second half of act two getting them out.

Consider your options. You already know your protagonist's needs, desires and fears, so what is the ultimate pit of despair that you can place them in?

According to Vogler, the turning point at the end of act two may be the moment of great crisis. (Vogler 1999, p. 162). The act two turning point may also be a redemptive moment, when the protagonist seizes the solution, the clue or the tool that will allow them eventual success in the climactic confrontation at the end of the final act. Syd Field suggests that the second act turning point is the time for a major confrontation between the protagonist and a support role. (Field 1984, p. 122). Either way, this turning point represents a moment of commitment for the protagonist, a time when they find a way of seizing control of the action.

For example, in *Thelma & Louise*, the act two turning point occurs when the two women use weapons to overpower a police officer who is about to arrest them. They seize his gun and use it against him, forcing him into the trunk of his car. Their use of these weapons allows the women to continue their flight from the law.

In act two, it is crucial to remember that all scenes must help carry the story forward towards an inevitable conclusion. There is some time for you to take us into the 'world' of a support character. You may take us aside from the main plot, or A-line, to show us a new realm. You might show the realm of the love interest (the B-line). You might also show us that of the bad-guy boss (the C-line).

When you have got your protagonist in the pit of despair at the mid-point, ensure that this situation reflects the kind of fear or anxiety you set up back at the beginning of act one. The underlying purpose of all scenes must still be in line with your overall premise and your overall narrative goal—to illustrate how the protagonist handles their central dramatic problem. Whatever you establish in act one as the protagonist's greatest fear will materialise at the mid-point.

Raise the stakes again, using various action points as levers. Let's say that you are developing act two of your urban romantic comedy. For instance, maybe the protagonist has a problem with both her job and her romance. She may lose her job if she can't complete an important work report on time. The added sting in this dilemma concerns this deadline. Your protagonist is *under pressure* to complete a difficult report at work. She is also *under pressure* from her boyfriend, who has scheduled a birthday dinner for the evening her work report is due (barriers, complication, deadline).

The deadline arrives and the protagonist runs from work to the restaurant but falls into an open manhole and breaks her leg (barrier and complication). She then gets trapped underground with a broken leg. At this point she may lose her job and her boyfriend and her freedom and her leg all in the course of one terrible mid-point (barrier, complication, reversal). The audience experiences great suspense, wondering how the protagonist can meet her deadline.

Whatever act two trials you choose for your protagonist, each needs to build towards the final climax in act three. The redemption of the protagonist is the business of the conclusion and will be dealt with in the next chapter.

EXERCISE 11

Keep act two moving forward

11.1   Identify the mid-point and the second turning point of your story. Now identify at least six scenes that shape the conflict. Build up to your key turning points using the following obstacles:

- barriers
- complications
- reversals

Remember that obstacles can come out of any or all of the following:

- the antagonist
- the love interest
- the secondary character's cross-purpose objectives
- deadlines
- revelations
- the protagonist's mental, physical or emotional state, including:
  - –survival issues
  - –health issues
  - –safety and security issues
  - –love, bonding and belonging issues
  - –esteem and self-respect issues
  - –success and achievement issues
  - –personal responsibilities
  - –inner conflicts
  - –relational conflicts
  - –social responsibilities
  - –situational conflict

11.2 Read a screenplay or view a movie in the genre that interests you. Focus on act two and identify the devices used to structure the mid-point and act two turning point, including:

- the barriers
- the complications
- the reversals
- the mid-point of despair
- the second turning point

11.3 Comment on the effectiveness or otherwise of each.

11.4 Compare these various approaches to your own screenplay outline.

12

Act three structure

Chapter objective

To shape the structure of act three through examining the processes of climax, 'pay-off' and resolution.

We have noted that the first half of act two is about digging the protagonist into a 'pit of despair', and the second half is about helping them find or fight for a way out of the pit. We have examined the way dramatic conflict is created by developing obstacles for the protagonist in the form of barriers, complications and reversals.

In this chapter, we will explore the structure of act three, examining the processes of climax, 'pay-off' and resolution. This is where the writer must finally prove the premise that has driven the entire story.

Writers often talk about the conclusion of a screenplay as if the story finishes with their grand finale. Our purpose, however, is to be more detailed and specific in our understanding of story structure. For that reason, we break the ending of the story into two distinct phases: the climax and the resolution.

A screenplay of classic proportions needs to be finished off in two stages or steps, not just one. The climax is represented in Step 6 of your outline. This is followed by a brief aftermath or, as the French call it, the denouement, which finally resolves the story. This resolution is an extremely important outcome of the story and requires its own place in the outline—the final step, number 7.

Without a convincing ending, the audience will leave the cinema feeling frustrated and dissatisfied. So, a good screenwriter must resolve their story such that the key themes and plotlines are all 'tied up', or at least accounted for.

From the audience's viewpoint, this means that all key questions raised in the story must be answered and all key characters accounted for and paid off. Steps 6 and 7 of your outline need to achieve this.

Focusing on the sixth and seventh steps will help you to nail down the themes and subplots of the story. The sixth step relates to the content of the climax, where all the outcomes of the main dramatic problem are addressed. Step 7 describes the aftermath of the climax. This is where you resolve the protagonist's problem to the total satisfaction of the audience.

Act three—step 6: The climax, or act three turning point

Step 6, the climax, usually brings together the protagonist's key problem and the central conflicts in a major scene of confrontation.

Note that the secondary characters and subplots must not be 'left hanging', with no outcome provided for their stories.

Go back to your subplot chart and your outline and ensure that you have dealt with the main characters' objectives, the central problem, and their main fears. Establish clearly what changes they need to make in order to deal with this confrontation.

You should by now have a very clear idea of the climax that will bring the dramatic problem to its peak and bring the protagonist into conflict with the key support roles. This climactic scene of conflict is step 6 in your seven-step outline. It provides you with a dramatic opportunity to really prove your premise. Whatever goal or aim you have given your protagonist in act one, it should be clearly shown whether or not they have achieved that goal in the final steps of your outline. Whatever idea has driven your story forward should reach full development by the end of the piece.

Act three—step 7: The final resolution

Step 7 of your outline represents the resolution, or denouement. This scene will finish or pay off the entire story so that the narrative is now closed. It represents the real, emotional outcome of the climax. This final passage of the story indicates to the audience the protagonist's *response to the climax*. It may also look forward in time, to indicate a sense of the protagonist's ongoing future direction.

The resolution is often structured as an epilogue that occurs some time after the climax. It may be set some moments after the climax, or it may stretch the story chronology some time into the future—even years down the storytelling track.

As with all key turning points of your story, the moments after the climactic turning point reveal much crucial information about the protagonist. The way in which the protagonist responds to the high drama of the turning points reveals their inner character. This is especially the case with the ending, where the protagonist's eventual response signals how they have resolved the problems of the story. From this final scene, the audience is to understand how the protagonist has resolved all their issues and how they will face the future.

At this final point in the story, the protagonist's dramatic problem needs to be resolved or fully explained to the audience such that there are no nagging questions or doubts about the outcomes.

To achieve this sense of total story closure, look back at the initial goals/needs/desires of your main character and decide which of these are fulfilled or negated.

Balancing the set-up with the resolution

As a rule, the resolution should deal in a clear-cut way with the initial problem. Look back at sentences one and two of your outline. This will help you to focus on what the final outcomes actually mean to the protagonist.

Good writers often structure a kind of symmetry between the ending scenes and the beginning scenes. After all, the goals, fears, dreams and problems that they begin with need to be addressed in a resolute way by the ending. Sometimes the protagonist appears to end up in the same place where they began. By thinking carefully about the contrast between the beginning and ending, it is possible to convey quite subtle things about a character. Maybe they have changed in some ways but not in others: they may end up in the same old house but with a new attitude.

Most importantly, all of the main outcomes of the story must make sense in the end. The protagonist's central problem drives the plot and gives it shape. This problem must be resolved in one way or another. This doesn't mean it has to be solved with a perfectly neat or 'happy' ending, but rather that all the issues the writer has set up for the protagonist to tackle are dealt with.

The protagonist's final gestures will prove or disprove whatever the writer has been trying to tell us all along.

- What larger view about human behaviour, philosophy or morals might you express through the mood of the ending?
- Have you expressed your premise clearly in these scenes?

Audience tension and release

In most genres, especially drama, comedy and adventure, a sense of redemption will be one overall aim of your protagonist's ending. This means that by the end of the story, your protagonist has partially resolved their problem or can at least look forward to some ray of hope in the future.

In the old-fashioned Hollywood ending, the protagonist would inevitably achieve some kind of enlightened or more highly evolved state. This was usually expressed through the attainment of love, of wisdom or of riches and material success.

It is technically breaking with convention to end the story with your protagonist in a lower or more dismal place than where we first meet them. This upsets the process of catharsis, which is a process of tension and release.

How does catharsis work? The audience identify themselves with the protagonist. As discussed in chapter 1, the writer must ensure that the audience grow to like, or even to love, the protagonist. They therefore experience a sense of tension when the character experiences trauma or conflict, and a sense of release or relief when the character achieves redemption.

Part of this process is the resolution of trauma and the release of tension that usually occurs at the main conflict points of the story. When the protagonist pulls through to survive various challenges, there is a renewal of hope in the audience. When the protagonist achieves fulfilment, it fuels the audience's elation.

In the Hollywood industry, it is known as 'box office suicide' to block this process of tension and release. This suggests that a dismal story, where the protagonist fails to achieve redemption or hope, may disappoint the audience by thwarting their basic needs. The audience feel cheated or frustrated, as their hopes are smashed along with the protagonist's. This can spell failure at the box office, as such stories are rarely a positive viewing experience. Audiences don't recommend dismal or depressing stories to their friends. Remember the needs of your audience. Their 'real' life is hard enough. Anthropologists suggest that part of the storyteller's job may be to provide creative, life-affirming strategies within an entertaining package. The way you end your story will reflect on your ideals as an artist and may encourage a sense of hope (or of hopeless nihilism) in your audience.

The need for redemption

Our need for a redemptive ending is part of a tradition that goes back to ancient mythology. Myths and legends about the heroes and heroines of tribal lore, fairytales, and folk and religious stories the world over have conditioned us to see great stories as messages about the need for persistence, courage and faith.

As a writer, your job requries you to create characters we can be inspired by. Whether we are discussing Goldilocks, the Buddha, the god Horus, Joan of Arc, the goddess Venus, or the knights and queens and warriors of old, mythical, literary and cinematic characters continue to traverse the ages, representing the human will to carry on, despite the great trials and pains that punctuate their journey.

If you recognise yourself as part of this ancient tradition, you might think of your protagonist as a slightly idealised human who represents the best and worst of us all but who, in the end, needs to triumph (at least partially) over the problems and circumstances of fate and psychology. The audience needs to believe this or they may walk away from your story feeling frustrated and cynical.

Your story need not end with roses, but take care that you offer the audience some wise observation about humanity, some pearl of moral insight or humour that they can take out of the cinema and reflect on. Consider how your premise is really the foundation of your entire story. A really satisfying ending depends on the existence of a premise that has been properly thought through and expressed in the various events and images of your screenplay.

It is clear that the days of the Hollywood 'happy ending' are over. The narrative style that ended with the cowboy or cop hero riding off into a golden sunset belongs to the period of great Hollywood-driven optimism—the mid-20th century.

It is worth observing that in most narrative genres, the protagonist's arc traditionally embraces a redemptive sense of growth, of enlightenment and of hope for the future. Various global traditions in storytelling show us a protagonist who may not find total success. Usually there is a price to pay for survival, or for wealth, or for victory in war. Rather than total success, the timeless protagonist finds redemption—the capacity to find hope, growth and enlightenment, despite pain, problems and discouragement.

Ironic or tragic endings are perhaps best handled within the genres of black comedy or high tragedy. Both of these genres are governed by very specific rules and require the writer to maintain their ironic tone with particular mastery.

One daring technical strategy is to rearrange the chronology of the story so that *if* the protagonist actually dies (which is to break the cardinal rule) this is not *seen* to happen in the final moments. For example, in *Thelma & Louise*, the two heroines decide to take their own lives and drive their car over a cliff with the police in pursuit. The film's final shot is of them sailing triumphantly into the blue; *not* crashing on to the canyon floor below.

In *Pulp Fiction*, gangster Vincent is shot at around the second act plot point. The action takes a backward step: we flash back to a moment earlier the same day and stay with this new chronology which concludes act three with a comic scene of Vincent and his partner triumphing over a couple of hoodlums. Their victory is made poignant and ironic as we realise that Vincent is actually to die shortly afterwards on this same day.

In *American Beauty*, the protagonist is shot dead in the climax, but we have known from the start that he is speaking to us from 'above'. His voiceover continues through the denouement, suggesting that he has found even greater happiness and redemption in another realm. In these examples, the death of the protagonist is managed in such a way that the audience is able to transcend the disappointment of losing their main point of identification. The result is a less 'downbeat' story arc.

In general however, for the purposes of most genres it is a firm rule to keep your protagonist alive. They are the audience's main point of identification: the audience's eyes and ears on the action. The writer must show the protagonist struggle towards the resolution of their goal. Tragedy and black comedy are genres which may allow exceptions to this rule. Tragedy and black comedy are flipsides of the same coin. They represent the twin masks of ancient theatrical tradition. These are perhaps the most challenging genres to work in. When a writer bends the norms and conventions of our moral universe they may either delight or offend the audience.

Examples of how to conclude your story

The kind of narrative under discussion here is placed firmly within the humanist tradition of arts, literature and philosophy. One premise of this tradition is that in the course of our struggles, we all may lose something (love or riches or happiness), but if we fight for our beliefs, we will gain something in exchange—understanding, wisdom, maturity or redemption.

This suggests that your protagonist may not achieve *all* their goals or solve *all* their problems but they may try to do so and may learn something in the process. The results are bound to be satisfying for the audience, as this is a human process we all can relate to. Struggle and strife are universal human conditions, after all.

Consider how the mood or tone of the ending can express your philosophical, spiritual or moral stance. The premise, or the concept that guides your story, will be proven or given full expression by *the relationship between your first and final scenes*. How? These scenes combine to depict the nature and magnitude of the change that takes place in your protagonist. These scenes also provide the essential contrast in situation which illustrates just how and why your protagonist has changed.

Look at turning points from these examples and observe the interlocking nature of the set-up and the climax. How does the resolution suggest the future direction of the protagonist in each?

Sunset Boulevard

Screenplay by Billy Wylder, Charles Brackett and G. Marshman

Premise?

Sometimes a woman will kill a man if she can't have him to herself. Or, there is nothing tragic about being 50, unless you are trying to be 25.

Set-up

A young man is found by the press and police floating dead in the pool of a wealthy, former movie star. We flash back to the same man, Joe Gillis, as a penniless writer who is behind in his car payments.

Climax

1hour, 38 minutes

When Joe starts packing to leave the mansion, Norma threatens to shoot herself, but shoots him instead.

Resolution

1 hour 42 minutes

Joe floats dead in the pool as Norma poses for press cameras, which she thinks are movie cameras set to capture her performance in her latest film, *Salome*.

Thelma & Louise

Screenplay by Callie Khourie

Premise?
It's better to die free than to spend your life in prison.

Set-up
A hard-working waitress, Louise, and her best friend Thelma, a frustrated housewife, decide to skip their small, humdrum, Mid-Western American lives for a girls' weekend alone.

Climax
1hour, 50 minutes
The women are chased across country by police who force their old T-Bird right up against the edge of a deep canyon.

Resolution
1 hour, 59 minutes
Rather than surrender to the police, the two women decide to drive right off the canyon's edge into the blue beyond.

Basic Instinct

Screenplay by Joe Eszterhas

Premise?

Sometimes when the evidence gets complicated, a cop has to trust his instincts. But then again, he might be wrong, especially if he is in love with his number one suspect.

Set-up

When a former rock star and heavy cocaine user is killed by a beautiful blonde with an ice pick, Detective Nick Curran—bad boy of San Francisco's homicide squad—is called in to investigate.

Climax

1 hour, 50 minutes

Nick's partner and buddy is murdered, seemingly by Beth, who arrives on the scene to be shot dead by Nick.

Resolution

1 hour, 53 minutes

Nick goes home to find Catherine waiting for him, so they make love. But there is an ice pick under the bed. Will she use it?

Psycho

Screenplay by Joseph Stefano from a novel by Robert Bloch

Premise?

Guilt and repression can affect the mind so powerfully that we can convince ourselves we are actually someone else and thus remain free of responsibility.

Set-up

Marion Crane makes love with Sam, a divorced man with few prospects, in a cheap hotel before going to her job at a real estate office.

Climax

1 hour, 42 minutes

With Sam lying injured, Lila searches the Bates mansion alone and wanders into the basement where Norman attacks her with a knife, dressed as his dead mother.

Resolution

1 hour, 45 minutes

While Norman sits in jail, wrapped in a blanket, the police psychologist explains that the young man has been overcome by a severe personality disorder in which he believes he actually *is* his mother—the 'woman' who killed Marion and the detective—the woman he actually murdered as a child many years before.

EXERCISE 12

The climax

12.1 Go back to your subplot chart and your seven-step outline to develop scenes which answer the following questions about the climax:

- Does your protagonist achieve their main aim?
- Does your protagonist solve their central problem?
- Does your protagonist confront their main fears?
- How must they change in order to deal with this confrontation?

12.2 Make sure that you have answered the following questions by the end of your story:

- Does the protagonist change as a result of their journey?
- Are they in a different state of mind and/or body than when we first met them?
- Describe the scenes revealing change.
- Do all the key support characters also resolve their situations—do they achieve their goals in relation to the protagonist?
- Do these resolutions happen in the same scenes where the protagonist changes?
- Are all plotlines closed off satisfactorily?
- Have all questions and issues raised in your outline been answered or addressed by the final three plot points of your story?
- How will you construct the solutions within character and situation?

12.3 Consider carefully how you want the audience to feel as they are walking out of the cinema.

12.4 What is the arc of experience that your protagonist needs to travel through between the beginning and the end of the story?

- How does the protagonist's psychology at the end of the story differ from their psychology at the beginning?
- What has the protagonist learned about themself by the end of the story?
- What concept or premise do you wish the protagonist's journey to 'prove' or reveal to the audience?

12.5 Let's review the seven-step outlines of the film examples presented in Chapter 6. In each example, note how the climax follows on directly and logically from the previous turning points:

- *Breakfast at Tiffany's*
- *Sunset Boulevard*
- *Thelma & Louise*
- *Basic Instinct*
- *Psycho*

12.6 Discussion: Reread the screenplay or view act three of one of the films you have already studied and identify the following elements:

- Which scenes build up to and include the climax?
- Which scenes pay off the climax with a satisfactory resolution?
- Are all the characters satisfactorily paid off?

Fleshing out your screenplay

In the previous chapter we examined the structure of act three, which includes the crisis (step 6) and the resolution (step 7) from the seven-step outline. In this chapter, we will construct a plot breakdown from your seven key turning points. We will then construct a scene breakdown from your plot breakdown.

At this stage of the process you should already have sketched out all the key elements of your story in your journal. The plot breakdown provides the writer with a vision of the big picture—the overall story you are trying to tell. The scene breakdown will detail all the layers of scene action and intention.

Fleshing out the contours of your seven-step outline

When the seven-step outline is completed, there are two more developmental stages before you start writing your screenplay: the plot breakdown and the scene breakdown.

- A *plot breakdown* is built upon your seven key turning points and briefly outlines every scene, its characters and action. It enables you to keep track of the story chronology and the purpose of each scene in relation to your protagonist, plot, dramatic problem and premise.

- A *scene breakdown* is a more refined version of the plot breakdown and contains all the essential information about every scene. It includes set-up information, pay-off information, character revelation, running gags, thematic images, mood and stunts. It does *not* include the dialogue.

Working on your plot breakdown encourages you to think and plan ahead. It gives you an overview of the whole of the protagonist's journey. It forces you to consider the logical problems associated with your concept. It reveals potential story problems early and allows you to rethink them now, rather than encounter them at page 60 of your first draft.

Your scene breakdown develops from the plot breakdown and allows you to plot out the many varied details of your story—except the dialogue, which can go in a separate journal. Developing a scene breakdown allows you to 'rehearse' your screenplay before you execute it. It is a scale model of the first draft that allows you to anticipate and solve problems in miniature.

The plot breakdown

At this early stage of writing your screenplay, you may not know exactly what happens in each scene, but you may have an idea about the larger structural purpose of key scenes which you explored in the seven-step outline. Now we can focus on the plot breakdown, which allows you to consider *where* each scene takes place and *who* will be present. Use it to keep in touch with structural issues and story elements. Remember, you will only be able to complete the breakdown if you already have a story outline in your journal.

Make your plot breakdown entries brief. Rather than cluttering up the plot breakdown with long descriptions, you need to keep the number of words to a minimum. This allows you to focus on the purpose of the scene and to read your story easily.

To begin your plot breakdown, on a large sheet of paper add several headings as shown in Table 13.1: page number, scene number, time, location, characters and action. Under each heading,

Table 13.1 Example of plot breakdown

Page no.	Scene no.	Time	Location	Characters	Action
1	1	Mon. Day	Pool	Jane	Jane swims laps
2	2	Mon. Day	Office	Jane & Jim	Working on design project
4	3	Mon. Night	Home	Jane & Randall	Falls asleep in front of TV
6***	**4*****	**Tues. Day**	**Office**	**Jane & Boss**	**Boss gives Jane a deadline*****
7	5	Tues. Night	Café	Jane & Randall	Randall suggests a holiday weekend
9	6	Tues. Night	Home	Jane	Jane stays up late working
10	7	Wed. Day	Airport	Jane & Boss	Fly to Sydney
12	8	Wed. Day	Office	Jane & Boss	Jane & Boss draw up plans
14	9	Wed. Night	Airport	Jane & Randall	Randall meets Jane and loses baggage
15***	**10*****	**Wed. Night**	**Home**	**Jane & Randall**	**Jane & Randall fight about her work*****
16	11	Thur. Day	Home	Jane	Jane wakes alone and upset

* Note that turning points are marked in bold and with asterisks. This helps the writer get a sense of the rhythm of the unfolding sequences and events.

231

you will create a list of all your scenes, including the essential information about who is in the scene, where it occurs, whether it occurs during the day or at night, and the key action or content of the scene. This provides you with an organised template from which you will create the more detailed scene breakdown.

A note about page: scene ratios

It may seem strange to decide ahead of time how long a scene is or to guess what page it might end up on, but it is important to consider how long you think it will take to get your information across succinctly.

Do some research into the length of scenes and the length of the screenplay you wish to write. Figure out the length of your key scenes and how these balance with the overall length of your screenplay. One helpful rule of thumb is to consider that the average number of pages per scene is about 1.5. This means ten pages of screenplay (or ten minutes of screen-time) will consist of around six or seven scenes at one-and-a-half pages each.

Consider how long you want your screenplay to be. More than two hours is too long. Some film producers and film finance agencies set rules about the length of screenplays they will assess. For some, 110 pages is the limit. For your own sake, try to keep it brief and set yourself an absolute limit. You don't want to write 300 pages and then have to cut it back. Aim to be concise.

Pacing your plot breakdown

Use your plot breakdown to calculate or estimate the number of scenes and pages you need between each turning point in your seven-step outline. Consider where and how you will introduce various subplots and how you can use them to build conflict, tension and suspense into the action.

Consider the following points to help get the most dramatic effect from your story:

Protagonist and problem

1. How can you increase pressure on the protagonist?
2. How can you intensify their dramatic problem?
3. How can you escalate the conflicts that you have established in act one?
4. How can you keep adding more problems and obstacles to the mix in act two?

Plot and premise

1. Clearly establish the protagonist's main aim and main problem in act one.
2. Create a deadline and raise the stakes.
3. Move the story forward using 'action points'—the barrier, complication and reversal.
4. Cut scenes that don't advance the story forward.

Try to envisage how your protagonist behaves and appears at the most extreme points of their personality. These points may be the start and end points, or they may fall at other turning points. Focus on key scenes you may want to sketch in as a way of understanding the arc of your protagonist. Refer to your journal to remind yourself of all your story goals and themes.

Now consider how you need to set up and pay off each turning point, and begin to sketch-in the full story as you go. By looking at their position within the entire framework of your story, your turning-point scenes will help you to arrange and pace all your other scenes.

For example, take another look at Table 13.1. Your inciting incident needs to happen at around pages 10–15, so you can put it there in your scene breakdown and mark it in bold or with asterisks. Now you have to set up this incident in the ten pages (six or seven scenes) leading up to it. You then need to pay off the inciting incident in the pages between this scene and the next key turning point at the end of act one.

The plot breakdown isn't a place for you to go into great detail about each scene—save that for the scene breakdown. The space devoted to 'content' should allow you to give a brief sketch of the scene. You don't need to figure out every single action and idea in every single scene. However, you do need to focus on the purpose of the scene—how it relates to the larger general direction of the protagonist's journey.

Try to keep all information about each scene on one line only— be brief and the breakdown will soon take the shape of a graph that allows you to judge the time between each scene and the relationships between different acts. In this way, the plot breakdown helps to keep you in touch with your larger structural purposes.

Mapping the plot breakdown

Once you have completed the plot breakdown, you can use it to trouble-shoot many aspects of your plot. For instance, you can begin to analyse your breakdown for specific visual and plot issues.

You can use your computer, or simply mark your paperwork with coloured pens to highlight certain aspects of content and chronology.

For instance, when creating the plot breakdown, it helps to mark out the turning points in bold or in another colour (say, red or blue) so that they stand out visually as key markers in the long list of scenes. That way, you have a means of estimating visually whether the chronology of your story is conforming to a classical structural form. For instance, you might discover that there are 40 pages between the first act turning point and the mid-point. This would indicate that the progress of act two is far too slow.

You can also keep track of your chronology by simply marking and observing all the daytime and night-time scenes. This will help you to get an instant picture of the balance between day and night, light and dark, in the story.

- What is the time frame that supports these changes as your protagonist shifts from one state to the other? Days, weeks, years?
- Do the number of days and nights add up to a coherent chronology?
- Are there too many day/night scenes?

These notes also allow you quickly to check the order and content of your scenes, ensuring that the story doesn't 'wander away' into a subplot realm or get carried away with a supporting character.

You might mark all those scenes that include a reference to the central problem. This allows you to chart the progress of your protagonist, keeping track of the way they are dealing with their problem and moving through their arc.

You can also keep track of subplots by marking in scenes that include various support roles. For instance, you might mark all scenes where the love interest appears, or you might discover a gap between the mid-point and the climax which doesn't contain enough references to such a key character or theme.

In this way, the plot breakdown provides a simple visual tool that allows you to explore and discover potential opportunities and problems in plot, chronology and action.

The scene breakdown

To begin your scene breakdown, take each turning-point scene from your plot outline and add more details, as shown in table 13.2. Then do the same for all scenes inbetween.

Table 13.2   Example of scene breakdown

Page no.	Scene no.	Location	Characters	Action & Purpose
1	1	Pool	Jane	Jane swims • Set up her independence • Set up running gag re car
2	2	Office	Jane & Jim	Working on design project • Set up boyfriend and boss demanding her time
4	3	Home	Jane & Randall	Falls asleep by TV • Set up lifestyle via furniture and her wardrobe • Set up conflict with Randall
6	4	Office	Jane & Boss	Boss gives Jane deadline • build on problems with boss • reveal Jane's aggression

You are not writing dialogue in the scene breakdown, although it may be handy to keep a notebook by your side so that when you come up with dialogue ideas you can jot them down immediately.

The plot breakdown will help you to shape and track the main story by keeping tabs on your main plot and turning points. The scene breakdown is more detailed. It enables you to consider specific images, actions and situations within the main plot and subplots. You can revise this scene breakdown and balance it by moving the dot-points to other scenes as you see fit.

Even when you get to the scene breakdown stage, you may still be in doubt about the exact content of a scene. Continue by jotting down the function of the scene: 'Set up theme A here', or 'Pay off protagonist's work incident with a joke'. If you flag your main intentions now, the means of achieving your aims will reveal themselves later as you continue to revise your outline.

The plot breakdown and scene breakdown may take you some considerable time. Don't try to rush the process: it will involve a lot of problem-solving. You may work and rework your scene breakdown and use it to create the contours of your plot. Once you have completed this process, however, the act of writing your screenplay becomes very easy. You have already committed to the protagonist, plot, dramatic problem and premise, and now have a clear map to guide you.

Summary and conclusions

We have seen how the plot or main storyline results from the nature of the protagonist, both inner and outer. The figure of the protagonist has a highly complex function, reflecting both the character of the audience and that of the writer. If the audience can identify with the protagonist and relate to the dramatic problem at hand, they are more likely to invest in the story as a whole.

To ensure all of this, the writer needs to know their protagonist as if they were a close friend. The protagonist must be an appealing character whose psychology and motivation is defined by a key dramatic problem. This problem moves the plot forward, using action, events and situations that prove or illustrate a series of themes. These technical elements are unified under the premise, which represents the heart and soul of the story (and of the writer)—the central unifying concept or philosophy that governs its various themes.

To construct the outlines of their onscreen world, the writer needs to consider various realms of action and conflict—both physical and psychological. The protagonist's character will also be shaped by the rules of the genre or the type of story.

When writing the backstory or character biography for your protagonist, consider how their external or physicial 'world' can help you to structure conflict within your plot. Use your journal to capture these ideas on paper.

An exploration of character backstory will help the writer to articulate the key dramatic problem that will drive the plot forward. The protagonist's problem allows the writer to crystallise ideas and themes around a particular set of images, character types and locations. Within this framework, the protagonist must undergo a kind of obstacle course in order to achieve their aims and goals:

- Dramatic problems can emerge from the clash between various realms in which the protagonist moves.
- Conflict can arise when needs and desires are confused.
- Conflict can arise when fear or foibles prevent the protagonist from getting what they want or need.

We have considered the plot as a kind of schedule or timetable of actions, dilemmas and events for the protagonist to deal with. When considering chronology, it is useful to differentiate between the time frame that the protagonist 'inhabits' and the 'real' time frame inhabited by the audience.

The writer must organise the entire plot, which describes relations between onscreen characters, locations and events within a mere hour or two of screen-time. The plot is organised around a logical sense of cause-and-effect such that the audience can see and understand how different events lead to different outcomes, consequences and effects. To manage all this, the writer must be aware of how genre can help to regulate the audience's appetite for comedy, drama, tension and conflict. The two main vehicles for the creation of all onscreen drama are the dialogue and action.

The writer may also be guided in decisions about characters and locations by referring to an overall premise, or concept. Consider which themes you will explore, as these can 'hook' the audience and get their interest. Remember that your story needs to be timely—it must have relevance to today's audience and may even refer to issues that are current or topical. Alternatively, it may refer to a classic, eternal or timeless set of themes and still have great significance to the here and now.

While the technical process of screenwriting can be sketched in a book like this one, the real learning comes from doing. Most importantly, get into the habit of daily writing. Keep checking and discussing your ideas with others to make sure you have an audience who can help you answer the big questions—So what? Who cares? When you have two or three good, polished scripts in your hand, the time will be right to find a producer. In the meantime, keep generating pages and remember the fire in the belly!

EXERCISE 13

The scene breakdown

Note: Even while you are busy on your scene breakdown, you may be inspired to start writing scenes and getting a feel for the tone of your dialogue and characters. Perhaps you will be tempted to begin with scene one, act one and move forward in a straight line. However, it may be wise to consider the entire arc of your story and to stay focused on the relation between the beginning, middle and ending. For that reason, you may also attempt to write scenes from later parts of the story.

Begin the first version of your scene breakdown. Focus on the protagonist's arc or emotional journey.

- How does the protagonist we meet in the first five or ten minutes of the story relate to the protagonist we conclude with in turning point 6 or 7 of your outline?
- How does the protagonist behave at the mid-point when they may be at their most weak and vulnerable?
- Use each scene to 'pay off' or resolve plot points we have just seen and to build towards or 'set up' the next turning point.
- Keep the chain of cause-and-effect in motion.
- Keep an eye on your page:scene ratio and figure out how the 'time of the tale' is progressing in relation to the 'time of the telling'. Remember, an average scene may equal 1.5 pages.

References and recommended reading

Aristotle 1997, *Poetics* (trans. Heath Malcolm), The Penguin Group

Aronson, Linda 2000, *Scriptwriting Updated* Allen & Unwin, Sydney

Bordwell, David and Thompson, Kristin 2001, *Film Art: An introduction*, McGraw-Hill Publishing Company

Buñuel, Luis 1978, 'Poetry and Cinema' in Joan Mellen, *The World of Luis Buñuel*, Oxford University Press, New York

Campbell, Joseph 1990, *The Hero with a Thousand Faces*, Princeton University Press, Princeton, New Jersey

Egri, Lajos 1972, *The Art of Dramatic Writing: Its basis in the creative interpretation of human motives*, Touchstone Books, Simon & Schuster, New York

Eisenstein, Sergei 1970, *The Film Sense*, Faber, London

Eisner, Lotte 1973, *The Haunted Screen*, Secker and Warburg, London

Field, Syd 1984, *Screenplay: The foundations of screenwriting*, Dell Books, New York

Field, Syd 1984, *The Screenwriter's Workbook*, Dell Books, New York

Jung, Carl 1975, *Man and His Symbols*, Doubleday, New York

Levi-Strauss, Claude 1976, *The Savage Mind*, Weidenfeld and Nicolson, London

McKee, Robert 1997, *Story: Substance, structure, style and the principles of screenwriting*, HarperCollins, New York

Maslow, Abraham 1970, *Motivation and Personality*, Harper and Row, New York

Mellen, Joan (ed.) 1978, *The World of Luis Buñuel*, Oxford University Press, New York

Seger, Linda 1990, *Creating Unforgettable Characters*, Henry Holt & Co., New York

Seger, Linda 1994, *Making a Good Script Great*, Samuel French, Los Angeles

Vogler, Christopher 1999, *The Writer's Journey: Mythic structure for storytellers & screenwriters*, Pan MacMillan, London

Filmography

ADAPTATION (USA/2002)
Screenplay by Charlie Kaufman
AMERICAN BEAUTY (USA/1999)
Screenplay by Allan Ball
APOCALYPSE NOW (USA/1979)
Screenplay by John Milius, Francis Ford Coppola
Suggested by the novella *Heart of Darkness* by Joseph Conrad
AROUND THE WORLD IN 80 DAYS (USA/1956)
Screenplay by S.J. Perelman, John Farrow, James Poe
Original story by Jules Verne
A TIME FOR DRUNKEN HORSES (IRAN/1999)
Screenplay by Bahman Ghobadi
AUSTIN POWERS: THE SPY WHO SHAGGED ME (USA/1999)
Screenplay by Mike Myers, Michael McCullers
BACK TO THE FUTURE (USA/1985)
Screenplay by Robert Zemeckis, Bob Gale

BANDIT QUEEN (INDIA/1994)

Screenplay by Mala Sen

BASIC INSTINCT (USA/1992)

Written by Joe Eszterhas

BLADERUNNER (USA/1982)

Screenplay by Hampton Fancher, David Peoples

Based on the novel *Do Androids Dream of Electric Sheep?*, by Philip K. Dick

BREAKFAST AT TIFFANY'S (USA/1961)

Screenplay by George Axelrod

Based on the noved by Truman Capote

THE CRYING GAME (IRELAND/1992)

Screenplay by Neil Jordan

DAVID COPPERFIELD (UK/1935)

Screenplay by Howard Estabrook, Hugh Walpole

Based on Charles Dickens' novel

DAVID COPPERFIELD (UK/1970)

Screenplay by Jack Pulman

Based on Charles Dickens' novel

DAVID COPPERFIELD (UK/1997)

Adapted for television by Adrian Hodges

Based on Charles Dickens' novel

DIRTY HARRY (USA/1971)

Screenplay by R.M. Fink, Harry Julian Fink

DR JEKYLL AND MR HYDE (UK/1932)

Screenplay by Samuel Hoffenstien, Percy Heath

DR STRANGELOVE; OR, HOW I LEARNED TO STOP WORRYING AND LOVE THE BOMB (UK/1964)

Screenplay by Stanley Kubrick, Terry Southern, Peter George

Based on the novel *Red Alert*, by Peter George

THE DOPPELGANGER
(see *The Student of Prague*)
GANDHI (UK/1982)
Screenplay by John Briley
THE GODFATHER (USA/1972)
Screenplay by Francis Ford Coppola, Mario Puzo
Based on the novel by Mario Puzo
THE GREAT DICTATOR (USA/1940)
Screenplay by Charles Chaplin
HIGH NOON (USA/1952)
Screenplay by Carl Foreman
Loosely adapted from a *Colliers Magazine* story, 'The Tin Star',
by John W. Cunningham
IN THE NICK OF TIME (USA/1995)
Screenplay by Patrick Sheane Duncan
JACOB'S LADDER (USA/1990)
Screenplay by Bruce Joel Rubin
LIMELIGHT (USA/1951)
Screenplay by Charles Chaplin
THE LORD OF THE RINGS: THE FELLOWSHIP OF THE RING
(NEW ZEALAND/2000)
Screenplay by Fran Walsh, Phillipa Boyens, Peter Jackson
Based on the J.R.R. Tolkien novel
THE MATRIX (USA/1996)
Screenplay by Larry and Andy Wachowski
MR SMITH GOES TO WASHINGTON (USA/1939)
Written by Sidney Buchman
Based on a story by Lewis R. Foster
MRS DOUBTFIRE (USA/1993)
Screenplay by Randi Mayem Singer, Leslie Dixon
Based on the novel *Alias Mrs Doubtfire*, by Anne Fine

OUT OF AFRICA (US/1985)
Screenplay by Kurt Luedtke
Based on *Out of Africa*, by Isak Dinesen
PARENTHOOD (USA/1989)
Written by Lowell Ganz, Babaloo Mandel
THE PLAYER (USA/1992)
Screenplay by Michael Tolkin
Based on the novel by Michael Tolkin
PRISCILLA QUEEN OF THE DESERT (AUSTRALIA/1993)
Screenplay by Stephan Elliot
PSYCHO (USA/1960)
Screenplay by Joseph Stefano
Based on the novel by Robert Bloch
PULP FICTION (USA/1994)
Written by Quentin Tarantino
Based on stories by Quentin Tarantino and Roger Avary
RAIN MAN (USA/1988)
Written by Ronald Bass, Barry Morrow
RUN LOLA RUN (GERMANY/1999)
Screenplay by Tom Tykwer
SAVING PRIVATE RYAN (USA/1998)
Screenplay by Robert Rodat, Frank Darabont
SCREAM (USA/1996)
Screenplay by Kevin Williamson
THE SHAWSHANK REDEMPTION (USA/1994)
Screenplay by Frank Darabont
Based on the story by Stephen King
THE SILENCE OF THE LAMBS (USA/1992)
Screenplay by Ted Tally
Based on the novel by Thomas Harris

SLIDING DOORS (USA/1998)
Screenplay by Peter Howitt
SOLARIS (RUSSIA/1972)
Screenplay by Andre Tarkovsky
Based on the novel by Stanislaw Lem
STAR WARS (USA/1977)
Screenplay by George Lucas
A STREETCAR NAMED DESIRE (USA/1951)
Screenplay by Oscar Saul and Tennessee Williams
Based on Tennessee Williams' play
THE STUDENT OF PRAGUE a.k.a. The DOPPELGANGER
(GERMANY/1913)
Screenplay by Hanns Heinz Ewers
THE STUDENT OF PRAGUE (GERMANY/1926)
Directed by Henrik Galeen
THE STUDENT OF PRAGUE (GERMANY/1936)
Directed by Arthur Robison
SUNSET BOULEVARD (USA/1950)
Screenplay by Charles Brackett, Billy Wilder, D.M. Marshman, Jr
Based on the story 'A Can of Beans', by Charles Brackett and Billy
Wilder
THE TERMINATOR (USA/1984)
Written by James Cameron, Gale Anne Hurd
THELMA & LOUISE (USA/1991)
Screenplay by Callie Khouri
WORKING GIRL (USA/1988)
Screenplay by Kevin Wade

Index